OUTSIDE HERSELF

Searched For Fulfillment, Found Purpose

Sahara Patrickson Forbes

OUTSIDE HERSELF. Copyright © 2021. Sahara Patrickson Forbes. All Rights Reserved.

Printed in the United States of America.

No portion of this book may be reproduced, stored in a retrieval system, or transmitted in any form or by any means, except for brief quotations in printed reviews, without the prior written permission of DayeLight Publishers or Sahara Patrickson Forbes.

Published by

DAYELight
PUBLISHERS

ISBN: 978-1-953759-66-5 (paperback)

At one point I wanted to write a book, seeking a solution to my problem. I never knew I am the solution.

Table of Contents

Chapter 1 7
Chapter 2 15
Chapter 3 21
Chapter 4 27
Chapter 5 35
Chapter 6 41
Chapter 7 45
Chapter 8 53
Chapter 9 57
Chapter 10 65
Chapter 11 71
Chapter 12 77
Chapter 13 85
Chapter 14 93
Chapter 15 101
Chapter 16 111
Chapter 17 117
Chapter 18 125
Chapter 19 133
Chapter 20 141
Chapter 21 151

Chapter 22	159
Chapter 23	167
Chapter 24	175
Chapter 25	183
Chapter 26	197
Chapter 27	203
Unprecedented	211
Acknowledgement	217

Chapter 1

I came into existence in human form in the early eighties; I am the first fruit of my mother's womb. I was born yellow and had freckles all over, which my mother brought to the doctor's attention. I was born at the community clinic so after they examined me, I was taken to the nearest hospital where they found out I had jaundice. I was given an injection and sent home. My mother continued treating me at home with cerasee tea and putting me to lie in the morning sun until it seemed like it had dissipated.

I remember living with my parents, my brother, and my father's parents, which would be my grandparents. My brother and I would play in our room at nights and play with neighbouring kids in the daytime. I attended a basic school which was nearby.

My grandmother, Miss Merial, would take me to church with her on Saturdays. She would normally bring an egg sandwich in a brown paper bag for me to eat during break time, which is still a taste I can remember. My grandfather, John Patrickson, was blind and had straight silver hair with a bald spot on top of his head. He would usually sit at one spot near a window smelling like every ointment for pain and speak with rhyming words.

Sometime after my parents separated, my mother took me and left my brother behind. We moved to a house where she lived when I was born. My great grandparents and cousins were living there.

It was a small-legged house on a hill. Originally it was a two-bedroom house that sandwiched the dining room, then an extra bedroom was subsequently added which my mom and I shared. A family plot was on the periphery of the small property near the latrine that we used, and the kitchen was separated from the house on the opposite side. The houses on the hill were some distance apart. The nearest one to us was like family; I would go over there to play or to stay when my mother was not around.

There was not much to do, so I would run around and catch bees that landed on the flowers for food, and sometimes I would make stick dolls from a particular plant called leaf of life, before I started getting real dolls. My great grandmother would put these leaves on her head and wrap them with a cloth to keep them from falling. Other times my two male cousins and I—we were all around the same age and lived in the same house—would wander away into bushes. One day we wandered so far that we heard what sounded like a lion's roar. We ran so fast that we were out of breath when we got home.

There were also times we would go looking for mangoes and other seasonal fruits. I remember this specific mango tree on the side of a steep hill; we had to use our hands for support to climb to the tree. The mangoes this tree bore had a unique taste; they call it milky. I have never tasted a mango like it again.

There were two girls next door, one was my age and the other was a little younger. I can remember that one of them used to walk in her sleep. I do not think they liked to play as much as I did. The girl who was my age was mostly in the kitchen; she started cooking from an early age. She was obsessed with eating; it was almost as if she was eating herself away and always seemed to be hungry. She would eat the flesh that was barely left on the skin of a roasted breadfruit as well as the bagged animal feeding that looked like cheerios. I tasted it once and it was not enticing.

One evening she had too much to eat so they had to roll her from side to side. I did not understand why they were doing it, but I stood there watching for a while. I then turned and walked away. I am not sure how long her discomfort lasted. A piece of zinc that was lying on the ground cut my foot, so I left and went home.

One night I was left alone in my room; a usual practice of my mother. It was a full moon, the place was well lit by the moonlight; it was so bright it felt like we were close to it. I laid there staring as usual at a stain in the ceiling that appeared to form a man sitting on a dog (it was my company), when I glimpsed something at the window. I immediately turned and saw a shadow in shape of a man, who appeared to be wearing a jacket and a fedora hat, looking through the window at me. I tried to figure out who he was, but he seemed strange; he almost looked like my great grandfather who I barely knew who had died not too long ago. I remember watching my grandfather lie in his bed on his back while his foot slowly slid down in comfort of his last breath.

I started to feel so afraid, I covered myself with a blanket of fear and continued to stare at him until I slowly drove into deep slumber.

My mother always appeared to be angry with me; she would beat me for everything, then tell me to "shut up" when I started crying, even when I thought I was right. This left me confused and thinking I was always wrong, so I shied away from being open with her. I was even afraid to tell her when I was hungry because I felt like it was wrong, so I would just go to sleep instead. I was molested by an older neighbor and a family member and I did not tell her; I kept everything to myself. My older neighbor touched me more than once, maybe about three times. It was a sweet touch that left me wanting more; it was the only thing that felt good in life to me. I knew it was wrong because he hid each time he did it, but I did not tell anyone.

I started writing little poems to comfort myself. At the time I was doing really well in school. I was attending the Adventist private school and I was a top student in my class. One day I sat with a blank paper ready to write but nothing came to mind. I started to feel like the house was watching me when I was not facing it, so I started living in fear, confusion, and doubt. I was scared of being alone; even though people were around me, I felt disconnected from them. I felt lonely, like I was in a world all by myself. It was a sad home with no light. No one celebrated anything, not even birthdays; every day was the same.

I started to spend summer holidays with my grandmother in the city. I remember one night I looked up and saw the moon and wondered why the moon was following me. I felt deeply as if someone inside was telling me that I am the chosen one. I thought to myself, am I going to be the next Jesus? I then asked God, "Why me?" But as time passed, I realized that the one moon is everywhere so I may not be a chosen one.

I loved being in the city. There were lights everywhere. My grandmother would take me across the road where she used to have conversations with a lady while I stood there watching the cars and people pass by. On Sundays, everyone would be home, and my grandmother would cook a traditional Sunday breakfast and dinner. I did not eat much, she had to force me to eat and while she was feeding me, I would find somewhere on my body to scratch. My body was always itching anyway from the heat rashes because the city was hot; it was like hell with lights. I remember they had to keep letting my hair loose. I had a lot of hair on my head so they kept pulling it out thinking it would have helped in some way.

On Sunday mornings you would hear different persons passing by selling newspapers, eggs, and brooms. They would be shouting and stretching out the name of the item they were selling as a means of advertising and to simply get people's attention, "gleeeaaanor, freeessssh eegggsss, broooom brooooom!" I always ran to the gate to look at them.

In the evening my uncle would buy me ice cream and my grandmother would sometimes go visit other family members. We would have to walk a distance to take a specific number bus that passed their community. My eyes would be as busy as the streets.

I remember one Sunday when my grandmother went to look for one of her brothers. We were sitting in his house when he started cursing and telling her that his father is not hers and she started crying. They said my great grandmother had cheated and got pregnant with my grandmother, so they treated her as such, along with her children and grandchildren. That is the reason I did not feel like we were a family back home; my mother and I were treated as if we were outsiders too. It is so weird that I was the only great grandchild that my great grandmother dreamt about. She told my mother exactly how I looked; she was blind before her great grandchildren were born.

My mother did not receive any love or affection, so she grew up having to defend and support herself. She stopped going to school at the age of fifteen after a stone rolled on the house she was living in. Everyone thought she was dead, but she was buried under the house. They found her alive with a broken leg after digging through the rubble, then they took her to the hospital. Her mother left her a few months after and moved to the city. She told her mother that she wanted to be a nurse and asked if she could come to school in the city, but her mother said no.

I remember my grandmother would take me to a particular yard a few times in the mornings. When we entered the yard, we had to walk around a pond which was in the middle of the yard. My grandmother would throw coins in the pond then sit and wait for a lady to come. We were always the only ones there as if it was an appointment. When the lady finally came, she would sit in front of us. She would start to write on a paper as if she was a two-year-old; I could not understand what she was writing but she would talk to my grandmother while she wrote. I remember she told my grandmother that my stepmother was working witchcraft on me, then I received a bath in some different kinds of bushes and cream soda. After the bath I had to put my clothes on without drying off, and then she gave my grandmother a date when to return.

Chapter 2

As I grew older, I started to feel empty and cursed. I still felt like I was never right, especially because I was still being beaten. I remember once I had little bruises on my face and my mother told me that if anyone asked what happened I should tell them I fell and hit my face on the bedhead. I was constantly being beaten and I just could not understand why she would not talk to me. I did not know right from wrong. I started to believe that what the woman said about my stepmother was true.

I started searching for something to fill the gap and I felt like love was the answer. I was not getting any at home, so I started looking for it on the outside; I started liking boys. I started writing again. I would sit in class and write love poems and drew a little heart on them. I remember writing one to a boy expressing myself, which was the only way I could because I was shy. My mother found it. She did not beat me that time, she just looked at me angrily and told me she should have let me die when I was little. When I was about two or three years old, she had to rush me to the hospital because I had a virus. I was dehydrated and looked like I was about die. From that day, I did not write another one.

Outside Herself

Then we were living on the main road off the hill with my little sister, brother, and stepfather. I was going to church on Sundays, and I was participating in Bible quizzes and competitions against other neighboring district churches; we always won. Sometimes I would keep church by myself or with my baby siblings when my mother was not around. I remember always singing Shirley Caesar's song "I Remember Mama" and tears would fall from my eyes.

My mother and stepfather would fight almost every Sunday; one would have a machete and the other an axe; it was very scary. Each time I thought my mother was going to die today. Even though I felt no love from her, she was the only one I had. I was so tired of the fights. One day, just as I reached to my father's side family reunion, I had to turn back. A man told me that my mom and stepfather was fighting. I went back home angry and went straight in his face and told him to stop fighting my mother. He pushed me down the steps. He used to molest me too. I would sometimes wake up from his touch, and it left me confused. When I turned to look at him, he would be near the closet looking like he was searching for something.

My father lived down the road from me, but it was like he was not there; half of the time he was in Canada on farm work. On his way from the airport each time he was coming home, he would shout my name and I would run down by his house the same night to pick up things that he brought for me. I would get a lot of candies and snacks so I would share with my friends at school the following day.

I had changed school too, I started going to a primary school about two miles away. I would walk back and forth every day. Other children from my community were going to the same school so I had company. I loved company. I never wanted to be alone. I remember the kids would talk about a teacher's niece that was in grade two before I started going there that the boys used to touch and I wished it was me.

Going to school was a rush. I remember trying to hop a van but fell. I got a big cut on my knee that needed stitches, but I went to the community dentist, pharmacist and doctor in one to dress it. Coming home from school was not so much of a rush; it was a bit slow and even slower when I had asthma attacks. I would have to slow down to catch my breath at times.

We would take our time when going home. Sometimes we would stop and pick fruits from people's trees and so on. One evening we got some ripe bananas from a market van. After eating them, someone asked what if the bananas were poisoned. The person went further to say anyone who did not burp was going to die. Everyone burped except me.

I dropped back on my performance in school. I could not focus as I used to, and I did not ask for help because I was still trying to think independently. I was really good at practical things like embroidery and playing games. I was one of the best players in just about every game: chiney skip, jacks, baseball, etc. We would play them during our lunch breaks. I was once elected as the 4H club president; I didn't know why they choose me. I had no idea what a president role was. On the theoretical side of learning, I was not doing my best. I knew I should be doing better but I just could not understand, and I could not focus. I

Outside Herself

would be busy thinking about what was happening at home and the future.

In grades five and six, I started to fight in school. I then took the Common Entrance Examination to go to high school; surprisingly, I passed. I spent two years in that high school then went to live with my uncle and his wife who I had never met.

That summer, before I left, my mom and I went to a wedding. Just as night fell, she sent me home to go light the lamp at home. I was scared to death to walk home that far alone in the dark and my stepfather had not too long died so I didn't even want to go in the dark house alone, but I couldn't tell my mom or she would have been mad and tell me to go anyway. She was not afraid. I had so much fear, I was even scared of the dogs in my yard. I remember coming from my neighbor's house one night and as I reach the gate, the dogs started barking and moving towards me. I started running and they started running me down as if I was a stranger. I ran so fast I did not feel my feet touching the ground, it felt like I was running in the air.

Anyway, on my way home to light the lamp I saw a guy I knew walking in front of me. I walked fast so I could catch him up. We walked and talked a little (I did not talk much; I was always a quiet girl) until he reached his house. He invited me in, and I went, then I realized he wanted to have sex with me, which I had never done before. I told him no and left. He then followed me and held me down trying to rape me. I did not scream for help. I felt a part of him stick me in my innocence and that was when I got the strength to fight and ran home. I didn't tell my mother because I know she would have blamed me for stopping by his house in the first place.

Chapter 3

I was now living with my uncle in Spanish Town and started to attend one of the best high schools in Kingston. I felt like a total stranger. They would take me to school and pick me up after. We would ride miles to school without saying a word. His wife was not that friendly; I did not know what to say to them and they hardly said anything to me.

I did not know anyone at school; I was just a country girl in a big city school. Learning was still a challenge. It was like the teachers were speaking an unfamiliar language. I could not understand anything; nothing stuck to my brain. All I did was sit at the back of the class with the boys wishing I could learn like the other girls. I hated school, I hated my life and I hated myself.

I started to focus on the outside. All I wanted to do was dress up; it was the only thing that made me feel better about myself even though dressing up was a struggle too because I did not have much clothes. I just could not wait to be an adult. I started to take jewelry from my uncle wife's jewelry box and wear them. I would do anything to feel good about myself. I started to skip school; I would just leave and return when it was close to dismissal.

One afternoon a guy from my community in the country called me and said he would love to stop by. He was a fairly decent guy. I think he was attending college at the time, and he was also living in Spanish Town so I gave him the address. At the time I was only being dropped off at school so I would find my way home. Sometimes my guardians would not come home until night, and I thought my uncle would not mind someone stopping by.

That afternoon the guy came, and we were there chatting a little until he started to touch me. I was surprised because I did not know he came for that. I told him to stop and also to leave before my uncle came home. He then held me down and I tried to fight him, so he only got the chance to put a hickey on my neck.

I went to school the next day and the vice principal saw the red spot on my neck and called my uncle. When I went home that evening, I sat there watching the news and as soon as the news was finished, I got up to go to my room but my uncle stood up and moved my blouse collar to look at my neck. He did not say anything to me. I went straight to my bed feeling so ashamed; I felt like I had let him down. I just wanted to disappear; no one had ever asked me what happen or why.

I packed my school bag with a few books and clothes then left. I could not look in my uncle's face again. All I needed was someone to hold me, talk to me and tell me they loved me. I wanted them to be proud of me but that was not the case, everyone thought I was a bad person and nothing I did was right. I could not even speak up for myself. I was dying inside.

I do not remember if I had been to school that day but that evening I ended up on Windward Road looking for somewhere to live. I just wanted to run away from life. It was getting dark so I told a lady who was nearest to me that I do not have anywhere to live and asked if I could come home with her. She asked, "Where are your parents?" I told her I was living with my father but he was away, so I was staying with my stepmother and she was ill-treating me; I lied to her. She said "Okay, but I live in St. Thomas" which was even better for me; the further the better.

I went home with the lady. She had two sons, one was named Mark and I cannot remember the name of her other son. I found out that she was a cyclist named Pauline or Paula. She was very desolate. We would eat baked dumpling every morning for breakfast. It was baked in a pot possibly because they could not afford oil. I do not remember if I had seen the boys go to school, even though it was coming to the end of the year; it was December.

I stayed there for approximately three weeks; I did not feel like I belonged there, and I missed my family. One evening I packed my bag and left without telling anyone. I went straight to the police station and told them I wanted to go home. They asked me where was home. I answered and they asked for a number to contact my parents. I gave them my uncle's number. They called my uncle and he said no. I then gave them my grandmother's number and she told them she would come for me in the morning, so they took me to the main police station that was in the capital. I stayed there on a hard wooden bench for the entire night. I could not wait for the morning to come because the place was cold and I was wearing only a skirt, t-shirt and a worn-out flip-flop and was being bothered by mosquitoes. The next day my grandmother came for me and bought me a new flip-flop. I put on the flip-flop, left the old one same place, and went on our journey home.

I continued going to school after the holidays while living with my grandmother. I went because I had to go, but for me it made no sense. Every morning I got up and got ready for school. I sat in class taking notes that I don't even understand. I couldn't grasp all of what they were teaching me; it was too much and I was still struggling to learn. My mind was cluttered and slowly disappearing from my head. I remember one day my form teacher, who was also our Physics teacher, stopped me and started praying for me. I do not know why he did it, but I guess he saw what no one else did. I needed it; nothing felt right to me, but that prayer apparently did not work because I was still feeling empty.

People in my community thought that I was this perfect, smart, and innocent girl. I remember a lady, who lived in the same yard and was like family to us, asked her daughter, who was also my best friend, why she could not be like me. I guess when you are silent, people think you are perfect. They did not even know that I was struggling to be myself.

My grandmother usually sent me to the shop to buy things to cook for dinner after I came home from school in the afternoons. One day, on my way to the shop, a guy held my hand, led me around the back of his yard where his room was and had sex with me. I did not even scream. He was older than I was. His brother was the one I liked; as a matter a fact, we liked each other. My first real kiss was with him, and we were around the same age. That night when we kissed, I was enjoying it. I closed my eyes and got lost in the moment, when I felt someone grab me; it was my grandmother. I was so frightened, it felt like I was in a dream. I ran under the cellar and hid; and didn't want to come out. I was so ashamed, I wished I could just disappear. Shortly after that he moved to live elsewhere.

Anyway, the guy had sex with me for a short moment then I left and continued my journey to the shop. I went back home as if nothing happened, and I did not tell anyone.

It was summer so school was almost out, and I was preparing to go and live with my mother so I could start going back to the high school I first started. I was fifteen at the time and while I was with my mother for the summer, I met a guy who she allowed me to date. I guess she liked him because he was a cute Indian guy from a good family. He would pick me up and we would go to parties.

One night I drank some alcohol and became so sick that I vomited everything I ate and drank that night. I started to feel weird in my body, but I could not tell why. I wondered if I was pregnant, but I did not know how someone felt when pregnant. I would squeeze my breast when I was in the bathroom and saw a little liquid coming out, but I was in denial. I wondered if having sex with a guy one time would have really gotten me pregnant; I refused to believe so. I did not know what to do or if it was my mind playing tricks on me. I had missed my period before for months because I had irregular periods, so I was not sure what was going on. I did not tell my mother because I did not want her to know I was not a virgin. It would be so uncomfortable to talk to her especially since I have never spoken to her about anything, and I had no one to talk to. I remember her asking me if I was pregnant because of certain things I was eating and I told her no.

I started going to school in September. I went to school up to November when my mom realized I was pregnant. We then met with the guy and his parents to discuss it but deep down I knew it was not his, but I wished it was. My mother then took me to a private doctor out of town and there she found out I was five months pregnant. I could see the color in her face drain into disappointment. I had disappointed someone again. "I'm so stupid!" I said to myself. I do not know why I kept silent all this time. I felt like disappearing. She then realized that it could not be his, so she asked who got me pregnant and I told her. This made her even more disappointed. Then I wanted to tell her that he raped me, but I wasn't sure if it was really rape because I didn't put up a fight or scream for help. She then called my grandmother and gave her the bad news, then told me I had to go back to Kingston so she bought me a few basic things and sent me back.

Chapter 4

Everyone knew I was pregnant and who the father was by the time I reached Kingston. That was when reality hit me that something was really inside of me, something I never even considered having no time soon and something I did not have control of. I did not see or hear anything from the baby's father. Maybe he was in shock too.

I stayed inside everyday feeling like I had disappointed everyone. About a month after, on a Sunday morning, I felt something running down my feet. I thought I was peeing myself when a cousin of mine who was staying at the house said that my water broke. She immediately called a cab; my grandmother was not there so I grabbed the few things I had and went to the hospital. I was not feeling any pain. I reached the hospital at 6 AM and gave birth to a baby boy approximately 25 minutes later. He was premature so he weighed 3lbs and 5oz. They immediately took the baby and placed him in an incubator. I stayed at the hospital the night, staring through the window wondering "What now?

Within the next two days, I was sent home without the baby. He stayed at the hospital for weeks, so I had to visit every other day to drop off diapers and anything they required. When the day finally came when I could take him home, it was a relief. I no longer had to go the hospital so often and I did not have a ride, so I was taking the bus and walking a good distance alone. I hated to be alone and to be seen on the outside.

The father came to look for the baby and he was there staring at him and asking why the baby's hair was so curly. There was a girl that was living with the people in the same yard I was living in who I had told about my cute Indian boyfriend, so I knew then that she had said something to someone about it.

Anyway, the father stopped by one night and told me he would start doing his part, which he started to do, even though it was just a little more than nothing and he only did it for a while, when he felt like, until his girlfriend who was living with him at the time got pregnant. Even though he was the one who got me pregnant, I did not treat him like he was obligated. I blamed myself; I thought it was my fault. His girlfriend hated me and my child because she thought her man and I had an affair. I still did not tell anyone what had happened; who would care anyway.

My baby father's girlfriend started to boast that her baby wears only name-brand clothing. She had people around her who could help, and she was working. In the ghetto it was all about name-brand things, but I kept my cool and I was busy in my mind as usual figuring out how to get to another level in my life. I wanted a job and I wanted to go back to school. Even though I had difficulty focusing, I was ambitious.

One day I took the baby to the hospital for his appointment; his routine checkup. I sat there, waiting in line for my name to be called when a nurse grabbed the baby and asked if I did not see that the baby was dying. I had no idea what she was talking about. Maybe I could not see that he was dying because I was also dying inside. I had to leave him at the hospital again for about a week or more.

He spent most of the time in the hospital and I spent most of my time stressing. We did not even get the chance to bond because he was in and out of the hospital for months. He was always in need of something such as blood and other things. I slept on the hospital benches when they started to admit him at the children's hospital. I was frustrated and tired; I could not handle it, I felt alone. I wanted to just leave my world, it was a world I did not want to live in; it was upside down or maybe not moving.

I met a guy and we started talking for a few days, then I went to his house and never wanted to leave. I stayed there for days. I could not stand my life anymore; I just wanted to run away as far as I could from myself, but I ended up going back home.

The baby started to sleep with my grandmother because when he slept with me, I would roll on him in my sleep. Months after, my grandmother and I had an argument and she told me to leave her house. I packed a bag and left. I did not know where I was going, I just started walking and thinking. She ran me out of a place I called home, even though it never felt like it. I was lost, walking in circles, looking for somewhere to live until night came.

I came upon a long road, it was dark and empty, not even a stray dog. I kept walking and wondering what was happening in my life. I thought about what my mother had said that she should have left me to die when I was a baby. I thought maybe she was right, and I really should have died because nothing seemed right. I was really not meant to be here so I would forever suffer.

I kept walking until I could see where the road ends, but it felt like forever to get to it. I felt like the world stopped and I was the only one moving, moving in slow motion. It felt like I was sleepwalking, but then someone grabbed me. It was a young man who then pulled me into a yard. The yard was on a gully bank, and it seemed as if he was a gunman camping, looking out for his enemies. He started to pull down my clothes and then raped me. It all happened really fast. After waking up, I pulled up my clothes, left the yard and continued on my journey as if nothing happened. I do not remember where I slept that night or maybe I went back to sleep.

I woke up the next morning at a bus stop. I sat there until a lady came and put out her stall, swept the area and sprinkled water all over for whatever reason, then packed the shelves with candies, snacks, and all that she was selling. I sat there as if I was waiting on a bus, but that bus never came. Now I was on the opposite side of time; the world was moving, and I was standing still. The only thing that moved was my mind. I thought about my baby for a short time; *I gave birth but I wasn't a mother*. I then started to think about my sad life again. Bad things always happened to me. I didn't even get the chance to choose who took my virginity and who to be the father of my child. I felt like I had no control over my life.

The bus stop was facing a lane. I sat there all day and watched the children playing happily in the streets as if they did not have a care in this world. I wished that I was a child again, or maybe not.

I barely remembered what had happened to me in the night, but my scent, since I had not showered, and tenderness reminded me that something happened. The day did not seem long as my time was fully occupied by thoughts.

When it started to get dark and the streetlights came on, it was time for me to move to find a safe place to sleep. I kept seeing a girl around my age or a little older walking back and forth as if she lived in the lane. So, I went over that side of the road and sat there for a while before asking her if I could stay with her because I had nowhere to sleep that night. She took me inside and her mother was there as well and her little sister. It was not a place I liked but I had to stay somewhere. It was a big yard with a lot of small, poor houses. I stood there looking around and it seemed like a place with no restrictions. People were shouting and speaking loudly to each other, and her mother did not ask who I was; it was kind of strange.

I told the girl I wanted to shower, which I did, then I saw her getting dressed. She said she was going to look for her boyfriend. I felt like I had to go with her because she had just allowed me inside her house, and I do not think she would have left me there as a stranger. So, I went even though I wished I could just go to sleep in a comfortable bed; I was just so tired from walking all night.

We walked about two miles that night. It was far but it seemed like nothing to her as she walked fast and was never tired. As soon as I reached where we were going, I had to sit and rest. It was another place in the ghetto but this time it was just one house in a big space; somewhere a little better than where she lived. She did her thing then we went back to her house.

I stayed there for a few days before I had to leave. One day a guy invited me inside his house and I went. He then locked the door and pushed me on the bed. I was surprised and I was like *"not again,"* then immediately I heard a hard knock on the door. When he opened it, it was another guy. The guy told him that he knew I was in there and he should let me out. The rapist went for a weapon because the guy insisted that he should let me out and they started to fight. That was when I got away; I went straight for my bag, left the yard and I never went back.

The girl had left and said she was going by her boyfriend, so I went straight there. It was a family yard; his mother, sister and brother were living there too. I stayed there, sleeping on the outside and sometimes sleeping on the sister's floor. I had to leave the room when she was leaving for work.

A guy named Ricky, also known as Scallawah, started to come there in the evenings. I guessed he realized I was just a stray, so he raped me more than once.

I then met a man, a bad man who ruled his turf. We became friends, his name was Ninja. He was the type that maybe liked his guns more than girls; he did not ask me for sex. I told him that a guy who usually comes in the yard raped me, and I was really afraid of him. He instructed me that whenever the guy returned, I should send someone to call him.

One night the guy came and started to deal with me badly because he wanted me to go with him so he could have sex with me. Shortly after I saw Ninja coming and I wondered who called him. Nevertheless, he came the right time. He started to hit guy with the gun telling him not to trouble me again. I found out afterwards that Ninja had arranged with the children who were living in the yard to come call him whenever the guy came and that was what they did.

A few days later, a number of police came by the house looking for me. I thought they were going to lock me up, but they were there to take me home. The girl and I had fallen out and she found my house and went there making a big excitement. Her boyfriend lied that I slept with him, but something had to happen for me to go back home.

Chapter 5

I was now back home but I was struggling with my body. Something was going on with my body that I was not sure about. I had a heavy discharge, but I kept it to myself. I did not tell anyone, and I did not have any money to go to the doctor.

My son's grandaunt, who lived in the yard but was living in another parish (St. Mary) at the time, took me and my baby to live with her; she had moved there not too long ago. She was living in one house with her man, baby, and my son. and her teenage daughter, who was the same age as me, and also my best friend was living up the road with her grandfather and that was where I stayed; we were back and forth between the two houses.

One day we went to a river and an older guy who my friend knew came by. His name was Ricky, also known as Scallawah, just like the guy who raped me back in Kingston. It was kind of strange that they had the same name and nickname, but they were not the same person. So, I was there playing in the water but I could not swim so I sat in the shallow part. The guy came and pulled me in the deepest part of the river. Even though I was fighting him, he still took me and let me go. I felt like this was the day I was going to die.

I went down in the water; I did not shout for help because I was busy fighting to save my own life. I came back up and was going back down when I felt someone grab me, it was the same guy. Apparently, he looked around because he was already leaving, and realized I was drowning and came back in time to save me. He took me out of the water, and then I lay on the sand for a little while in disbelief. I had the worst headache ever; felt like water had gone inside my head. After the whole ordeal I went home.

I lived there for about a year and still had the heavy discharge and didn't know what to do, still hadn't talked to anyone about it. Sometimes I thought that maybe it was normal, especially since it was said that everyone was made different.

Now we were back in Kingston, living with my grandmother. I remember I got some money from abroad from one of my cousins; she was the one who helped to take care of my grandmother financially. I decided to go and look for my mother because maybe I could talk to her now about what was going on with me, and it had been a while since I had seen her. So, I packed a little bag; I never had enough to pack a big bag and it was not my intention to stay long as I was busy looking for jobs.

It was late evening when I got there. The distance was about three hours' drive. I met my mother at the gate, and she started cursing that she did not want me there. She said she was going to take me to reform school, a school where bad teenagers went. I turned back, but it was getting late so I could not return to the city. I decided to go and sleep by the old house where I grew up. I still had that fear, so I went and asked a longtime friend of mine to come and sleep with me.

The next morning, I went back to my mother's house just to find out if she had anything she wanted to give me to give her mother. I could take it for her since I was leaving and that was where I lived.

As I arrived, I saw my mother sweeping the front yard. She seemed to be in the same mood as the night before so I stood at the gate and asked her if she had anything she would like to send for her mother. I don't remember if she answered. As I walked away, I could see my little sister standing on the step, piercing me with her big bright eyes, while tears formed in mine. I missed them so much, I felt like I was leaving a part of me there. I held back the tears because I did not want anyone to see me crying on the street. I have never allowed anyone to see me cry; they would think something was wrong with me, which was the case, but I have never expressed it. I was taught not to cry, and I was a big girl. The tears wanted to come out so bad, but I just could not let them.

I got lost in my thoughts on the bus; everyone seemed to be a stranger in my life. I was even a stranger to myself. Nothing felt right. All I wanted was to be a good person, but bad things kept happening to me and everyone thought I was bad; they could only see the bad.

Outside Herself

No one taught me what was right from what was wrong. No one was ever there to lead me on the right path; they only saw the wrong path I already took.

I went back home and wrote a letter to my mother saying that I was looking for a job and she should send my little sister to spend time with me. I still did not tell her what was going on with me; all I wanted to do was make her proud.

The city was a busy place; everyone was busy. People passed by doing their own thing, so no one heard or saw me. I felt so small; everyone around me were giants. I was too small to be seen, I was almost invisible. I screamed for help, but no one could hear me.

I felt like I skipped all my teenage years and jumped into adulthood. Now I would love to have a job, a car, and a house. I started to feel even more stressed because I did not know where to start. I did not have qualifications to even get a good job. I started looking for one because I had a child and myself to care for.

My grandmother's ex co-worker had opened a shop that sold oil, fuse, clamps, and other things for cars. It was a very small shop; I could barely turn in it and the pay was just as small. If I had bills to pay, I would not survive but I was grateful. I remember I was able to save and buy my son a tricycle and a cake for his second birthday. I also went to a school and paid to do CXC Mathematics and English for the first term. I went for that first term but failed to continue because I had no money and no one to ask for help. There was no one around me who was interested in education or could help, so I was on my own. I started to meet all different species of men as I was now being exposed in a bigger world by being on the road going to work, with men from all walks of life who wanted to get into my pants. I remember I met this young guy who would call my phone every morning and we would chat for long periods of time. I did not like him for having a relationship, but I liked his vibe. One day a girl called me asking for him, I was surprised. She said she was his girlfriend, but she had not seen or heard from him for a few days now. It was then I realized I had not heard from him either.

This guy's girlfriend started telling me about her boyfriend. The name I knew him as was not his real name and she got pregnant for him, but he caused her to lose it. He also did not have any family she knew about. I told her if I heard from him, I would let her know. A few days after she called me saying that she needed to go look for him. She seemed to genuinely care for him. I told her to come see me so I could give her something. By then I knew she barely had bus fare to continue her search and I was going to my mother for the holiday.

My mother was doing much better; she had opened a bar/shop and she was keeping a party then. I always preferred to spend my holidays in the country because I could see people and friends I had not seen for a while. So, I met the girl, and I gave her some money out of the little I had for bus fare and food so she could continue her search, then I headed off to the country. In the middle of the party, she called me to tell me that her boyfriend was dead; police had shot him.
The government buried him because he had no family that she

knew. It was sad; may his soul rest in peace.

The holiday was over, so I went back to my normal life, which I did not like. Whenever I left home to go anywhere, I felt heaviness over my body when it was time to go back. A man who hung out or worked up the road from my house took me to work most mornings. He was not a good-looking man but he seemed to always be available when I was going to work to offer me a ride. I was always happy to take the ride because the thing I hated the most and still do is to stand at a bus stop waiting for a bus; I never liked to be seen. Surprisingly he had never said anything to me as if he wanted to get personal; he was just a ride to work.

This man started teaching me to drive. I got a few lessons from him until I did not see him again; maybe I got too busy for him, or he did. It felt good driving so now I needed a car, but how? That was impossible based on what I was working. I started to date guys with money, which I still did not get because I was not the type to ask or demand anything.

I started to get frustrated; I needed another job because that job was not helping. I could not even buy the things I liked in terms of clothing. I liked nice, quality things; my standard was way higher than I could imagine, and I was only seventeen.

Chapter 6

I left the job and started working in bars. I made more money, but I never had the time to go to school because of the hours. Work began at ten in the morning and continued until late at nights.

I did not have any friends, so I would visit an old classmate of mine that was living out of my community. I went by her now and then whenever I felt like I wanted to leave home, which is how I always felt. I always felt like I wanted to move.

Her sister and I became friends; her name was Keisha; Keisha was very cool. I went back and forth a few times when I got my week off from work. While visiting them, I realized that Keisha was always going out of town and coming back with money. I was intrigued, so I told her I wanted to come, not knowing how she got it or even asking where, I was just ready.

I could not wait to make that money, I was hungry. She told me the day when she would be leaving so I packed my bag and went by her on that day. It seemed like she was taking forever to leave. I sat there all day waiting until she said she was leaving in the evening. Evening came so we went to the bus park and went on a bus to Montego Bay, the second city. I was excited.

We finally got there after about two and a half hours. It was now nightfall. I followed her on the busy streets; people were still on the streetside selling whatever they were selling. I remember she stopped and talked to a few women as if they knew each other. I was wondering how she knew these people in this big place. Anyway, we came up on this building where she went inside. It was a bar; we then went straight upstairs. I saw a few more girls there and the place did not look pleasant. Next, I saw Keisha putting her bags away and getting comfortable. I said to myself, *"O Jesus! Is this our destination?"* It was a strip club.

I wanted to go back home but it was too late, so I stayed. I decided that I was not going out there to dance. What if someone who knew me saw me? All kinds of thoughts started going through my head. I sat there looking and listening to the girls and I did not feel like I belonged there. They were rough, assertive, and, based on their conversation, I recognized they were doing this for a while. How could they be so comfortable with what they were doing? Keisha then asked me my name. I asked her what she meant. She explained that I could not use my real name in these kinds of places. The first name that came to my mind was Apple.

It was time to work, and I did not want to go out there, but a man who worked at the club said I could not stay if I was not working. So, I went and showered and put on some clothes. I do not even remember where I got a costume from, must have been from Keisha. My nerves were rackling as I walked slowly down the stairs. It was the slowest I have ever walked. I went straight onto the stage as I was instructed. The music was so loud, it was pumping in my chest. Not many people were there but the night was early so the vibe was not up as yet and it seemed like they made the amateurs go first. I stood there feeling naked, even though I partially was.

I stood there with my cute self, rocking in slow motion as the wave of the music pushed me left to right and fear kept holding me back. I felt so awkward; I did not even know what to do with my hands. I was so shy. I had no confidence. After having my child, my boobs dropped and dragged down my self-esteem. I hid behind myself then held on to the pole and stood there all night rocking as if the pole was a man. I could see Keisha's eyes wide open and her lips saying, "Dance!" I could not dance; I stood there wondering what the hell I was even doing here.

People started coming in. I was hoping not to see anyone I knew. Men started tipping me; I was the apple among the bunch, so everyone wanted to pick me. I made a lot of tips that night, so I decided to stay the entire week. I ended up spending about two weeks then I went back home. I did not go back. I used the money I made to send myself to Face Place where I learned to do nails and became a certified nail technician.

I rented a little space in a salon from a lady who did hairdressing at her home up the road from where I lived. I did her client's nails. I was there for a while before she told me that she was going away, and the shop would be closed. It felt good being my own boss, but I did not make any money; just enough to buy basic things and to pay the rent. I could not buy the products I used. So, I was back at square one; I was back at a place where I wished I had the right people in my life who could help me. I was all alone and on a job hunt again.

Chapter 7

I met a guy named Robert and we started dating. I was not sure what I liked about him, I was just lonely and bored, so I continued until we ended up in a relationship. I guess when you are lonely you hold on to anything.

After being in the relationship awhile, I found out that he was involved with a girl before we met who lived down the road from me in the same community. I do not normally go down that side and I knew his best friend was living down that side as well, so I thought it was just his hang out spot. I was not thinking of him having a relationship because we spent so much time together. He was always stopping by his grandparents' house as if he lived there, but he respected them enough not to take a girl there and I was okay with that.

We used to partially live at a hotel. I continued the relationship because I was enjoying his company and his job usually took him places out of town and I would go with him sometimes, which I enjoyed. I later found out that when he did not take me, he took the other girl. I confronted him about it, and he denied it. By then the girl had found out about me, but none of us left.

He then started to get controlling. I was getting afraid of him so I would try not to do anything to get him mad. One day I was in the middle of the street waiting on him while he was supervising a construction site and where I later found out that he actually lived, when I felt someone came up behind me. When I looked around, it was the other girl. I did not know her, but by the look on his face on his way to me, I knew she was the one. He said something to her, and she left. I then realized that she had stabbed me on my hand. I did not see when she did it because my back was turned, I only felt my hand getting weak and when I looked on my hand, I saw a tiny hole as if she had used an ice pick. Robert immediately took me to the hospital.

Sometime after, he invited me to his house, and I went even though it did not feel right knowing that the girl sometimes slept there. I passed the yard and knew that was where he was living but I had never been inside. Also, it had a gate so I could not see in the yard. Basically, I did not know what to expect. When I went in, I did not like the setting. There were some small rooms with an outside bathroom that everyone seemed to use.

I followed him to his room, and I looked around. I did not see any female things. He left me there and went to work so I was there alone for hours. I remember I wanted to urinate so badly, but I did not want to go outside to use the bathroom that everyone used and I did not want anyone to see me because I was too ashamed. I kept up my urine so long that I could no longer hold it. I then took one of his cups and passed my urine in it.

Later that day I fell asleep, and I dreamt that a fat woman came in the room and held me down. I could not move for a few seconds, then she went and picked up a bunch of keys and gave it to me. I left and never went back; obviously that woman knew I did not belong there and wanted me to leave. I am a dreamer; I dream every day, whether day or night, my whole life. It is like I live another life when I am asleep. As soon as I close my eyes, I cross over into another world. My dreams always meant something to me. I studied them; sometimes if something was going to happen, I dreamt about it. My grandmother was also a dreamer, and my mother. My mother was like the nurse she wanted to be in her dreams. She would normally dream about plants that are medicine.

One day after I was walking pass the house going about my business, I felt something hit me. It was the girlfriend; she hit me in my back with a bottle and ran behind the gate. I went home for a cutlass and headed back down the road to fight her. I did not tell anyone that I was going to fight. I hid the cutlass nearby in an old car because I did not really want to use it; I do not even know why I went for it.

Apparently, she knew I was coming back, or they saw me, so when I got there, her family and friends came out to defend her. Luckily one of my friends was coming along and he told me to go home, so I did. I would be stupid to even try to fight everyone and my friend would not have left me to fight anyway; he was determined to take me home.

The relationship by then was drifting apart or maybe I was the one drifting. I no longer wanted to be in that relationship, so in

Outside Herself

order to escape I went uptown sometimes at one of my male friend's house. I mostly had male friends then. Robert found out that I had been missing at times, so one night he came to my house and we were sitting on a bench under a cherry tree that was in the yard for hours talking. As soon as he realized everyone was gone to bed, he started punching my head as if he was in a boxing ring. As usual, I did not scream. A lady who was in the yard saw and immediately called my grandmother. As soon as my grandmother came out and started cursing him, he ran to his car and left. Others came out after hearing the noise. We stood outside talking and I almost passed out; I felt my body falling to the ground and someone held me before I fell. We then went to bed because it was late.

I wished he did not hit me because I missed being around him. No one had ever spent so much time with me, plus I dropped everyone when I met him. I started to go in the lane next door to hang out and started smoking marijuana. I normally buy it and ask a guy to make it for me, until he taught me. He said I needed to learn to make it and I should not let anyone build it for me, so I did. Marijuana then became my friend. I would hide around the lane and smoke every night.

Robert and I ended up talking again. I used to hide and meet him because we were too embarrassed to let anyone see us together. I told him I might be pregnant because I wanted attention. I was still feeling empty and lonely inside; I always needed to feel love. I did not love him, but it was the closest at the time because we spent a lot of time together. Even though I missed my period, which was normal for me at times, I was on an injection, but the contraceptive was not working too well with my body, so I started having bleeding problems.

One night, just after sex, I started bleeding. He got angry and said my grandmother took me to get rid of the baby. He did not know I lied to him, and I felt like it was too late to tell him, so I left it at that.

At that time, Robert had moved and lived uptown. One night I went to look for him and his girlfriend was there. She hid in the office and then found her way out for me not to see her. I pretended not to see her. At that moment, I realized she was more stupid than me. Why would she hide and she was his girlfriend first? I then got mad at him and went into his van and drove it into a wall. He got mad at me and pushed me, so I got a bruise on my back. We ended up spending the night together anyway.

Weeks passed; I was at my male friend's house uptown chilling; his name was Paul. Sometimes I would go by him when I wanted to clear my mind. He was hardly there because he worked long hours.

One Sunday, Paul was at work, so I decided to surprise him and cook rice and peas and chicken; the Jamaican traditional Sunday dinner. I was eighteen and never cooked but I had an idea how to. So, I went to the supermarket and purchased two of each item just in case I spoiled something and needed to start over.

On my way from the supermarket, I called Robert and a female answered his phone; it was his girlfriend. He was living close

Outside Herself

by where I was, but I did not let him know because that was my hiding spot. She gave him the phone and I asked who answered it. He said it was the helper. I asked him why the helper was in his room when he was sleeping and why she would answer his phone. He must have gone into the bathroom to talk to me because I heard the girl beating down the door and cursing.

I went home and told the taxi man not to leave. I was just going to put down my bags and let him drop me around the road by Robert's place. I took up a knife, went back in the taxi and told him where to take me. When I got there, his car was not there. I knew he had left to find me so he could tell me a story. I went in the yard and saw a female outside on her phone, it was his girlfriend. I was so happy to finally meet her, so I said, "OMG, you know how long I want to beat you!" She replied, "See me here!" then threw an empty bucket that was beside her at me. I then went over to her and started beating her really bad until I saw blood. I did not know how she was bleeding. I had the knife in my hand, but I was sure I did not deliberately cut her, but I did not stop. I started pulling her by her hair, then a guy who was living on the property ran out and started shouting that I must let her go and asked if I was going to kill her. I stopped and ran back into the cab and called Robert and told him I had just beaten his "gyal." I then went to my friend's place to cook as I planned.

I cooked the rice and peas, but it did not come out the way I expected. The peas were hard, and the rice was salt. So, I threw it away and started over. I could not wait for Paul to come home to eat. When I finished cooking, I went for a smoke while

I waited on him. I was excited and proud; it was my first meal; I did not even eat. I was waiting for us to eat together.

Paul finally came home. I told him I cooked dinner and he looked at me laughing and said okay. I went in the kitchen and shared his food and gave it to him. I sat there watching him to see what he was going to say, and he looked at me with a smile. I could see it in his face that he was forcing himself to eat it. I asked him how it was, and he said it was okay, but I knew he was lying. He only said it was okay so I would not feel bad, which I already did. I never cooked for him again.

Chapter 8

About a week or two after I went home and did not tell anyone about the fight, but everyone knew by now that Robert and I were not together. I did not want them to know that his girl and I was in a fight, so I kept it to myself. I still went by my friend, Paul, and had started a basic computer course in the evenings. One day, I was walking on the road and a car pulled up at my feet; it was Robert and the girl. He took me to the police station where they had made a report that I stabbed her in the head. I knew Robert did that to get back at me because he was not seeing me and thought I had moved on.

The police took me down to where the prison cell was. I thought they were going to lock me up, but they took my fingerprints and gave me a court date. I still did not tell anyone. When the court date came, I went and pleaded not guilty, and they released me on a $10,000 bail. I did not know what to do and I was afraid they would put me in jail. I went outside and saw a policewoman and told her what happened and asked her what was next, and what they meant by $10,000 bail. She explained that the judge was going to ask me to pay at least half of it so when I was coming back I should bring the money.

Outside Herself

I wondered where I was going to get the money from, especially since I was not working. The judge gave me another court date, and then I told my grandmother and others in my surroundings.

On the next court date, I was at Paul's house. I had asked him to loan me the money and he agreed. I stayed at his house so I could get the money and it was walking distance from his house to the court. He told me he would go get the money that day and drop it off before it was time for court.

It was coming to the time for court, and I had been calling Paul but not getting through. I started to get worried, as my anxiety starting to build. I then build a "splif" to smoke and turn a bottle of wine to my head. I kept watching the time and was continually calling Paul but still no answer.

It was almost time for me to go to court. It did not come to mind that maybe I did not have to go. I felt I had to deal with it so I could get over it and at the same time I did not want them to put me in jail. I got ready and started my journey in spite of not having any money because I was being obedient. I was drunk and high at the same time; you could see my eyes bleeding and fighting to stay open as my body got weak and I was stepping on air and moving past time. I reached in no time.

When I reached the courtyard, I saw everyone who lived in my yard. I was surprised to see so many of them. I felt happy on one hand but sad on the other. I was happy they came but I looked on them with the thought that not one of them could loan me the money.

I stood there for a short while before I went inside. I was so nervous; I went in and sat down thinking that I might have to plead not guilty again so the judge can give me another time to come to court. By then, I would get the money. I was worried that I would be going to jail that day. "I can't believe Paul did this to me. I thought we were friends. No one is ever there for me," I thought. Then I heard the judge call my name. I was startled, as I was lost in my thoughts and didn't expect her to call my case so soon. I think I peed myself a little, then I looked at the door and saw someone indicating that Paul was outside with the money. He came through at the last minute. I was so happy that I didn't even hear what the judge said. I just pleaded guilty. The judge asked the girl how much was her medical expense and she told her $5000. Someone gave me the money and I immediately handed it to her. The judge then placed me on one year probation. I had to report to the probation office once per month.

The girl and her friends started calling my phone threatening me. I told my probation officer and she said I should not do anything because if I commit another crime during my probation, I would go to jail. So, I kept my composure.

One day I saw her alone in the town. I was not going to do her anything as I did not want to get in any trouble. I remembered what the probation officer told me. I went over to her and asked if she wanted another beating. She did not say anything. I then walked away and from that day she has never called my phone again.

Chapter 9

One night I decided to go to a retro party uptown that I had heard advertising on the air. That same night I went to a tailor who was living in the lane for him to make me a skirt to wear. He made it in no time. I got dressed in it and tied an army-printed scarf around my breast as a top and put on a pair of boots I had and headed out. I was enjoying myself; I danced, it was a different atmosphere than what I was used to: nice music and nice people, the vibe was right, and I was feeling cute in my sexy army outfit looking like a Destiny's Child in the "I Am a Survivor" video. A man later came over to me and gave me a business card. It was a model agency.

I called the agency the following day. I was told when I could go by the office to sign up and meet with the manger. The manager's name was Judaz.

I started working with them, doing promotions. Working with them opened my eyes to another world, a world I wished I grew up in, even though the closer I got, the duller I felt; I couldn't shine amongst them. All the girls were beautiful, they were confident, they spoke properly, lived in good neighborhoods, had friends who were like them. Everything seemed to be perfect; they seemed to have the best parents. Some drove their own cars and were in good jobs; the promotion job was just a side job for them. I would just keep myself aloof, in a little corner doing my job to get paid and go back down to my little world in the ghetto. I didn't want them to know where I lived and that I already had a child.

I didn't work every day, so my time was flexible. Most nights my surrounding friends and I would play dominoes for hours; we loved it; it was our recreation. When I was not playing, I would be gone some place with my male friends, gone to have a drink and sometimes out of town. I was always ready to leave. Any opportunity I got, I would be gone because I liked male company; they were the only ones who took me places.

Sometime after, while playing dominoes, I realized a van normally slowed down for a few seconds then drove off. I remember my friends saying that it was me someone came to see. My friends knew that if a flashy vehicle came down on that road, more than likely, it was coming to me, plus this particular vehicle was slowing down close to where we were, but I did not know anyone who drove that colour vehicle and I could not see the person. The windows were tinted, and it was always night when the van passed by. I was normally into playing dominoes, so I did not have time to be figuring out who the person was. Sometimes I would see the van go around a street nearby.

One evening, while in the shower, I heard a girl I knew calling me. I was surprised and wondered what happened that she had to come straight into my house to call me; it was unusual for her. I answered and she said someone wanted to meet me. Immediately my mind ran on the van; I knew the van sometimes went around the street where she lived but I never knew who specifically it went to. Anyway, I told her I was in the shower and my hair was not in a condition to meet anyone. She said I should not worry about that, I must just come, so I said okay. She then left.

The person was by her house, so when I came out of the shower I put on my best casual outfit; a pink pants and a pink top, then left the house nervously. I did not know what to expect and I was shy; I wasn't sure how to act. As I turned the corner, I felt something leap inside. I could see him; he was standing on the sidewalk across the road from her house. I felt so awkward walking towards him, I was not even sure how to walk.

As I got closer to him, I got more nervous. He was standing there waiting for me. He was standing on one foot with the other on the wall behind him. His back was not leaning on the wall as other persons in that position would do. It looked like he practiced that pose or maybe he did not want his clothes to get dirty; either way, he looked perfect. I remember saying to myself, "Damn! Why does he want to meet me?"

I finally got to him; he was wearing white jeans, a white t-shirt with blue pattern and white sneakers. Everything about him was so clean and pure; he looked like God was in him. I looked up to him, since he was standing up on the sidewalk and I was standing on the road in front of him, then he introduced himself as Eddie. He had an accent, like a mix of Jamaican and

Outside Herself

American. He seemed shy too. I told tell him my name, then we exchanged numbers and went our separate ways.

I walked off, hoping he was not staring while I was walking. I could not wait to reach the corner so I could get out of his sight. The entire night I thought about seeing him again.

The next day he called and invited me to the movies. He came and picked me up in the night. When we got to the theater, all the movies had already started. Neither of us knew what time the movies started so we went to the drive-through theater a long distance away. When we got there, we did not want to stay because it looked like it was almost closed. So, we left and decided to go to Devon's House for ice cream instead.

After eating the ice cream, he said he was going home to change his shoes. I was wondering why but I did not ask. I asked him where he lived, and he said across the road, so I said okay. By then I was comfortable with him; we were together for about two hours talking and the girl who introduced us was a pretty decent girl, so I was comfortable enough to accompany him to his house.

When I got to his apartment, I sat on the couch, and he asked if I wanted something to drink. I asked him what he had, and he started listing so I told him a glass of champagne was fine. I sat there for a while drinking and watching television way more than the time someone would normally take to change their shoes. I then went down to his bedroom to ask him if everything was okay. He said yes and stood there looking at me as if he wanted to tell me something. I thought to myself that he could not want to have sex with me on our first date.

I turned to go back up to the living room when he asked me if I wanted money. I looked back wondering why he was asking me that. I needed money but I did not want to say yes because it was our first date. I thought about it for a few seconds then said yes. He asked me how much and I began to wonder why he was putting me on the spot; he could have just given me any amount he could afford.

I did not know how much to say because I had never told anyone the amount of money I needed before. I did not want to say too much to turn him off, so I told him $3000. He looked at me, laughed and said, "You're a good girl." He opened a draw full of money. It was the most money I had ever seen in one place. I wished I had said more. He gave me the amount I told him, then he took me home.

The next day I went shopping. I thought he might ask me out on another date, so I was preparing myself. I did not have enough money to buy what I really wanted, knowing my true standard and he was hot, but I searched until I found something that was nice and affordable.

The next evening, he stopped by me and gave me money to do my hair and nails, which I did. Two days later he invited me to the club; luckily, I had bought my outfit. He picked me up and I was so happy to see him. When we got to the club, we came out of the van, and he was so hot; he was like a caramel cookie that just came out of the oven. I was looking hot too. He was wearing an expensive jacket that looked like papers hanging off with signatures of Hollywood Stars on them. It was the first time I was seeing a blazer like that; I loved it. He took my hand, and we went into the club. There was a guy who knew him, so he let us inside; we did not have to join the line.

We went inside and met with two guys who stuck by us. I later realized that they were his friends and like his bodyguards. It was fun watching him dancing the "Log On." He wasn't a good dancer, and he didn't dance much either, we had that in common, and even more, we shared the same birth month too.

I gave a little cute flirty sexy dance every now and then, while sipping on champagne and hoping I could smoke a cigarette but kept my cool because he did not smoke.

The next day, he said he was going to take me shopping to buy me a white sexy outfit like the one Aliyah, the singer, wore in her music video, "Rock the Boat." I had a frame like her so he would call me Aliyah. Back then people called me all kinds of names, like Barbie, Modeler, and others.

I took him to a store I loved. That store was everything; they sold very unusual things that suited my personality, and they were of good quality. It was fun for him to watch me changed into different outfits. There was no limit to his money. I took bags home; even things I did not pick were in the bags, things he chose behind my back. When my grandmother saw the bags, she was upset and asked why I did not take the money instead, but I could not tell him that. How could someone who I just met offer me something and I tell the person I needed the money instead? Now this was the first time I felt happy in my life.

We started going places together, even soccer matches. He liked soccer and he even bought some guys in the area jersey outfits so they could make a team. It was a joy for me to watch him play. He had a good posture, and his profanity was like music to my ears.

We went to the club almost every week on ladies' night; we got VIP treatment. They even took his photo and put it in a magazine as a high roller with bottles of champagne in the club; he wasn't too pleased about it. He wasn't a guy who sought attention; I loved that about him. It was such a turn on for me. He was just always seen, and his presence felt, effortlessly.

We were always surrounded by girls, all kinds of girls, some were looking real good. They could hardly wait for me to take a bathroom break so they could flirt with him. Every girl wanted him. I stood by his side like a queen, on his high, looking down on the hungry girls ready to eat him, even my own friend. I remember him telling me that my friend came by his apartment to see him behind my back, but she could not get in without his consent. The security was the one who called him and told him who it was, but he did not let her in. I wasn't surprised; it was Keisha.

He later told me that his wife was coming to visit Jamaica. I didn't remember him telling me he was married. I was heartbroken. He had told me that he was deported for selling drugs and he was trying to get back in the country.

Outside Herself

Anyway, his wife came and was here for a while. I missed him so I decided to go the club one night. I knew he was going to be there. I regretted it. I saw him and his wife, she wasn't young and hot as me, but she was in the place where I would normally be. That was when I accepted that he was not mine and made up my mind to move on.

Chapter 10

I started a relationship with my child's father because I wanted to get over Eddie and he was the closest option. Also, he was my son's father, so maybe we could make life together, especially since he and his girlfriend had broken off at the time. I did not know much about him personally since we had never dated or anything, so starting the relationship was like getting to know him.

One day I saw a foreign number calling me and it was Eddie. He called to tell me that he finally got through and had left. I missed him so much, I was sad the entire day.

Eddie had been looking about to leave for a while from we were together. One night when I was visiting my mother, he called and said he wanted to see me before he left, and I should arrange my taxi man to give him a call so he could take him to the airport early in the morning. He said he got through and was leaving the next day, so he wanted to see me, but I was far away. I tried nonetheless. A friend who was visiting Jamaica from England was passing through St. Elizabeth from Montego Bay, so I told him I had to go to Kingston that night. I did not tell him why, so we decided to meet up so I could get a ride with them. We got there early morning, so I didn't get to see Eddie. I felt good trying.

Later that day he called and said he did not get through, so he had to come back home. I was kind of happy he did not get through even though I was still fighting to protect my heart. A part of me was happy and another part was sad because though I wanted him to stay, I would rather he left; that was where his life was, and he would be happy and I had already moved on. Eddie passed over a decade later. May his soul rest in peace.

I started sleeping at my son's father's house every night. One night he tried to hit me. I had a moisturizer tube in my hand, and I lifted my hand to block him from hitting me, so a point of the tube bottom cut me in my face. I had to go to the hospital that night to get it dressed. It left a scar beside my nose; every time I look in the mirror, I regret going there.

I lingered in the relationship, waiting for an opportunity to leave the community. I never felt like I belonged there. We had nothing in common and I wanted someone to uplift me, not someone who was on the same level or below me.

One night, when he was gone to a party, I packed the few things I had there and left. I went to live with an elder cousin of mine who I visited sometimes when I went by Keisha's house. It was just up the road from her in the same scheme. He was living alone because his children were grown and lived in America with his wife. He was glad for the company.

Not long after, I met a big man. He was a businessman in his fifties and at the time I was about twenty-two and was ready for a change, a new environment; it was like a breath of fresh air.

The big man was very kind. He started sending me to school and took care of me. My cousin and I were getting along. I would go shopping for food for the house and he would cook whatever I wanted. We would watch television and talk and laugh.

I was still smoking marijuana, so every evening after class I came home and built myself a spliff before bed. I hardly saw the big man because he was very busy. Occasionally he would take me to fancy restaurants as a date and I would spend the night at his place. He would drop off my money whenever he thought I needed it and when my school fee was due. We would just talk over the phone when he was not busy or when he was not sleeping. I think he had a sleeping problem; he used to fall asleep in no time, even at the stop lights, he had to always be drinking coffee to keep himself awake.

Months passed and I started to go to the club every now and then on ladies' night when I could afford to buy an outfit. The clothes Eddie bought me had disappeared; I hardly had a piece to show from his collection and it was only about two years after he left to go back to the States; they seemed to have disappeared with him.

I normally came home sick and had hang overs from drinking because I would leave my house without eating. I did not want my tummy to look big in my sexy outfits. I was really conscious of my tummy; it always had to be flat. My cousin used to tell me I got sick because I would not eat before I went drinking, which was true.

After deciding not to go to the club for a while, one night I just got up and decided to go. I was not sure if I should as I barely had friends but I knew I would probably see someone I knew or even meet someone new as I always did. I was not a bad looking chick, and I was still maintaining the same frame I always had. I never gained weight, which sometimes I wish I could, but it wasn't easy. Everything in my life was a challenge. I was still struggling to learn at school, and I could not gain a little weight, plus I was still feeling empty, so partying and dressing up served as a little ease for me. Even though going to the club sometimes did not even make sense, I would be in the club full of people and still feel lonely and sad. At times I felt like it was a waste making so much effort to buy an outfit and still not enjoy myself. I just could not understand why people around me seemed to be enjoying themselves and loving life. I would rather smoke a spliff and go to my bed.

When I got to the club, I saw a girl I knew from the school I was currently attending. We stuck together for the night. She did not seem to have any other friends there either. She was the party type. I always saw her every time I went to the club, and she had been in music videos dancing.

When it was my usual time to go home, I told her I was leaving and she asked, "Already?"

I told her it was almost time for the club to close anyway and she said, "Yeah, but when the club closes, everyone going downtown at another party."

"Downtown?" I asked.

She answered, "Yes, you should come!"

I thought about it for a little while, then said okay, since I did not have a job to go to the next day and my classes were in the evenings so I had all day to sleep. Maybe I was also a bit stuck up; it could not be that bad, so we went.

When we got there, a lot of persons who I saw at the club were there. People were in the middle of the road dancing and having fun, including a few celebrities. It was the area don who kept the party every week. I was a bit uncomfortable knowing that it was a bad man's party.

My friend started dancing immediately, like her life depended on it. I stood there looking around, forcing myself to relax. I was too shy to even walk across the road to the bar to buy myself a drink. A guy a little distance from me started trying to get my attention. He was not the hottest or the cutest guy, but I didn't mind having someone to talk to; at least that was something to do rather than standing there like a doll not doing anything.

The guy sent one of his friends over to ask if I wanted a drink. I thought about it for a second before saying okay. So, he asked what I wanted and went to get it.

When it was almost time to go home, I started wondering how I was going to get a ride since no taxis were parked outside like at the club. I asked my friend how we were reaching home and she said we could ask someone for a ride or take a cab. I said okay and immediately went over to the guy and asked if he could drop me home. He asked me where I lived and said no problem, especially since he was going that direction anyway.

On our way home, we met in a minor accident. The car was barely hit by another car in the back. It was a minor scrape, he said. I was too tired to even come out of the car to look. My feet were tired, and my eyes felt gritty. It felt like I had not slept for years. When I got home, it was daylight, and people were going to work. The guy and I exchanged numbers, then he waited until I got inside before driving off.

Chapter 11

The guy from the party called me later that day and we talked a little while, getting to know each other; his name was Patrick. Days went by and I found myself partying with this guy almost every night. I liked him; he was really fun to be around. I got hooked to his personality; he was like a boyfriend and a girlfriend in one. He used to tease me that I was boring because I don't dance, but now and then I would still do my little "stush" dance to songs I really liked.

Now that I had been spending all my time with him, I fell in love. I started to feel like I could not get enough of him. I wanted to be around him 24/7; he was now my world. I could not even breathe without him. Whenever he dropped me off, I felt like he left with a part of me. I just wanted him to come back in order to be myself. He would pick me up from school every night and on Fridays we would go eat roast fish on the roadside, which I had never done before but I liked it. It was different from going to the fancy restaurants that the big man usually took me. I felt like I could be myself around him, plus I liked the fish, it tasted good.

One night we went to the party where we met, and we were

there with his male friends. I was the only queen in the pack, so I stood out, a little distance in front of them, all dolled up in a short jeans skirt, a red heels, a tiny cute lady bug straw bag with a red and white stripe bow and a red top that marks, "Let's get dirty." I was looking good; yes, I was feeling myself.

While standing there, a celebrity came over and said I looked nice. I said thanks without a smile, and he walked away. I spent most nights at Patrick's house, which was some distance outside of town. That night/morning when we got home and got into the bedroom, he gave me one punch in my tummy. It was so hard that I bent over holding my tummy. He accused me of being involved with the celebrity, like he knew something I did not. I started crying while holding my tummy, then ran out of the house down in the bushes. He was so angry, I thought he was going to kill me. He ran and caught me and took me back to the house. I was so sad, I was there thinking to myself that this could not be happening; I loved him, and he just hit me, oh, how I was going to miss him. I laid there sadly in my thoughts wishing he had not hit me but was inside of me instead.

Later that day he took me home. I felt so heartbroken over his ignorant behavior, and I missed him so much. I sat there thinking about him every second of the day; there was no space to even think about anything else. It was like my heart replaced my mind. After maybe a day or two, I went back to him. The love for him healed my pain; once he was back, it was like that part of me returned.

I met a girl named Tanya at school at the time and we became good friends. Patrick hated her; he thought she was going to lead me astray. Maybe he knew that I was easily led astray, and he did not want to lose me.

One night Tanya and I went to the club; it was a Friday night "After Work Jam." I told Patrick we were going because it was a possibility I might see him. Tanya and I were on the top floor where a lot of big men were, dancing and having a good time. I could see the entrance from where I was standing. I saw Patrick when he came in, but I did not move from where I was because I was having fun. Shortly after, he came where I was and gave me a look that suggested he was here so I should leave where I was and come with him. Tanya already knew I was controlled by him; she hated him too. I followed him and stood with him. He was angry, so standing beside him broke my vibe. I decided that I was just going to go home.

I started planning my escape. I walked up on the top floor to go to the bathroom and then walked in the crowd on the bottom floor to the door so I could leave without him seeing. As soon as I went through the door, I felt someone grab me. I was so frightened, I started coughing. It seemed like he was watching me all along. He then led me to his car, put me in and drove off. I was thinking that this guy was going to kill me as he drove pass my community. I started crying, then he started cursing and asked what my plans were and why was I trying to escape. I told him I just wanted some fresh air. He drove straight to his house. His house was way out of town, so it took a while to get there. He did not hit me, so the night ended well.

We made love as usual, then went to sleep. He was great in

bed; he would kiss my heart of femininity and tell it how much he missed it, then make love to it passionately with his fresh breath and soft tongue while staring in my eyes. I wasn't confident to stare back in his so I would close mine, biting my lips, shivering, and moaning softly in pleasure. His passion for it turned me on and the love I had for him just could not wait for him to slowly force himself inside me, even though I did not like penetration. It was painful for me (I thought maybe I was born to be a lesbian); I just liked the fact that he was inside of me. We would make love all night until we fell asleep with him inside.

We would normally wake up in the afternoons, shower and stop on the way home to get food. He would ensure that I got home in time to get ready for classes. Most evenings I just had enough time to go change my clothes and pick up my books, so he would wait in the car on me so he could drop me at school in time, although I would rather stay with him.

One day, on the journey home, we were cruising and listening to Tevin Campbell's album, which I loved. Tears started flowing from my eyes. I looked at Patrick through the corner of my eyes wishing I could just hold him tight so he could melt into me and fill that empty space inside. He was so near, yet so far. The tears flowed even harder; I didn't want him to see me cry but I couldn't help it. He looked at me and asked me what happened and started laughing as if it was funny. He had no idea how empty I was inside. I dried my tears and kept silent. I began wondering if this feeling was normal; can someone love a person so much and still want more? This was like suicide. It was impossible to love him more. I thought loving someone that much would fill me. It felt wrong to love someone so much, but at the time it felt right, which left me confused

The big man was still in the picture. I was busy loving someone else and he was busy making money. I hardly saw him; he was more like a father to me. One night he was supposed to drop off some money and that same night Patrick was supposed to pick me up. I prayed they did not come at the same time; they didn't know of each other. I wanted the big man to come first because I needed the money.

My phone rang and I ran to answer it; it was Patrick calling to tell me he was at my gate. I became nervous; I started spinning around in the house not knowing what to do because I knew the big man was almost there too. Seconds after, I heard my phone ring, it was the big man, and the nervousness became worst. I did not know what to do.

A girl I met in the model agency was staying at my house at the time because her house was burned down, so I had asked my cousin if she could stay there for a short while. I told her I wanted her to go outside and collect something from someone for me, she said okay. Then I called back the big man and told him I had diarrhea so I was on the toilet. It was the first I had ever told someone I was on the toilet without feeling shy. I continued by telling him I was going to send my friend outside and he said okay. It was a relief. I went upstairs in my cousin's room so I could see what was going on without anyone seeing me but the mango tree near the balcony was blocking my view. So, I went in my room and waited until my friend came back in and the big man left before going outside to Patrick.

When I finally went outside to Patrick's car, he hit me and said he knew that vehicle came to me and not my friend. I didn't say anything. I then thought about leaving him because he was no use to me. I was with him yet I still had to depend on someone else to take care of me, but that thought did not last for long because I loved him.

Chapter 12

I did not tell Patrick about the big man. I thought he would have known because I was not working apart from doing promotions now and then, so someone would have to be taking care of me and I did not want him to think I was a cheater so it would be okay for him to cheat too, although that did not stop him.

One night Patrick was supposed to pick me up from school but called and said he would be coming in Kingston late so I should take a cab home, or I could wait. I told him I would wait, and he said okay. When class ended, I called him, and he said he was not in town as yet. That night my school friends and I decided to hang out for a while and get something to eat. While eating I could only think about Patrick; I was used to him picking me up in the evenings.

After we were finished eating, we were getting ready to go home so I called him again and did not get an answer. I was so upset, I just took a cab home. While I was home, Keisha called and asked me to come with her on the road. She said she had given a homeless woman a bag of callaloo with an envelope that her father had given her earlier that day when she went to look for him in prison. I told her okay since I was still upset for not getting through to Patrick and coming out of the house would maybe ease my mind a bit.

When I reached the area that she said the woman was, I saw Patrick's car in the theatre parking lot. I knew it was his car because it had a cute little "Reggae Boys" stuff doll that I bought and had put on the dashboard. I came out of the car to look at the license plate to be sure as I knew that license plate so well. I called and asked if he was still not in town, and he said no. I felt my heart skip a beat. I then looked at my watch and realized it was almost time for the movie to end. I waited to see who he was with. Not long after I saw him and his friend along with two girls coming out laughing and eating popcorn as if they had a great time. I stood beside the car feeling weak in my knees and my heart pounding, wondering if I should fight him or leave. As they came closer, I decided to leave because I was afraid to embarrass myself. I walked where he could see me and left.

I did not even know if my friend found what she came for nor I did I ask. My heart was broken, I went home, and I immediately lit a spliff like I usually do after school every night. That incident was not enough for me to move on, as he came later and told me that she was just a friend visiting from the states. As soon as my heart was back in line, or so it seemed, everything was okay again.

Another night my cousin who I was living with was away visiting his family in the states. I was left alone in the house so Keisha and another girl who was living two blocks from me came over and we sat in the back of my cousin's truck in the driveway chilling when Keisha decided we should go to a party nearby. This party was kept every week, but I had never been there. I never really went to a party without Patrick. The last time I told him I was going to a party with friends, he reached my house before I even put on my clothes to stop me from going. Anyway, we got ready and went. I got all dolled up in a ruffle backless top and white skirt with black embroidery that fell on my hips, showing my flat tummy, with my cute navel button that was cut just right.

As I entered the party, I saw Patrick with his friends and a different girl; we were both surprised. I walked over to him, with my cute self, and my friends by my side, knocking my dark silver iron shell purse with my medium length french tips.

"What are you doing here?" I asked Patrick, while swaying my hand left to right at him and the girl. I had seen her before in the club and I spilled my drink on her and she did nothing. That night he told me she was just a friend and I believed because I was the one who went home with him that night. My friends were there standing and watching what was going on. Keisha stood there staring at me with eyes that said if I wanted to fight, she was ready, but I was too cute to do that and I really wasn't a fighter. I didn't like to fight, but I would if I had to.

Patrick told me he was going to take the girl home and come back because he picked her up from her house. I said, "Hell no! Let her take a cab." He then walked to one of his friends. Shortly after I saw his friend coming towards me, he took me aside and said he wanted to talk to me, but then I realized

Patrick was missing. I asked him where was Patrick and he said Patrick had gone to drop the girl home. I felt so mad but did not show it as usual. His friend then explained to me that it was only fair to drop the girl home safely knowing that he was the one who gave her a ride there, and then I sort of felt a little better. Not long after, I saw Patrick returning and we finished the night together.

I did not know how my friends got home. Patrick took me home and we stayed up on the verandah until daylight. I did not invite him in because my cousin hated him. He thought Patrick was not good for me. I guess he was seeing my pain.

One evening, Patrick took me home after sleeping by his place so I could change my clothes and he could drop me at school. When I came back outside, I saw him talking to someone on my neighbour's balcony. It was weird because I never talked to anyone there. I was not that friendly. I would just say hello or good morning and go about my business, so I was surprised to see him having a conversation, worse with a smile. Then again, he wasn't that stuck up. Patrick was the type of person who would engage in conversations about sports and wasn't afraid to state his political views. But what could he possibly be talking to them about? I wondered. I looked up and saw a girl. She was my neighbour's friend who was a Jamaican living in Italy, so she was just visiting. It was the first time seeing him talking to someone there. Anyway, I ignored it, we went in the car and left for class.

Days later, as Patrick dropped me home and left, my cousin said that my boyfriend told the next door neighbor's friend that he slept with her sister.

I had told Patrick that one night I went to bed before my cousin, which was unusual. When I was in my room, I heard a strange noise like someone was having sex. I took my time and lay down on my tummy so I could look through the space between the stairs. There I saw my neighbor and my cousin having sex.

I could not even look in my cousin's face. The more I thought about it, the deeper I felt betrayed and hurt, I couldn't believe the man I loved did that to me. The guilt and shame came over me and covered me deeply. I left the house and thought I would go by Tanya's workplace; she was working at a restaurant as a waitress. I just wanted someone to talk to. As I left the house on my way to take a cab, a guy I knew stopped at my foot. I told him to drop me by my friend and he said okay. He started asking me about my friend and wanted to meet her. I was not in the mood, and he was not the type I would want her to meet anyway.

When I was almost at her workplace, I called her but did not get an answer. At the same time the guy kept pressuring me to meet her so I told him she was ugly so he would not want to meet her so he could stop bothering me. He then drove off and I went around the back where she would be. I saw her and she was mad saying, "Oh, I'm ugly?" I sat there a little while and realized she was really mad and avoiding me. I did not try to explain anything to her. I thought she was behaving immature knowing that she was not ugly, plus my heart was bleeding. She being mad with me about foolishness was the last thing I wanted right then so I left.

Outside Herself

I called another friend of mine named Saundra who I had known over the years but since I moved, I only saw her occasionally. She had met Patrick, in fact, she liked him. One day I saw her calling Patrick's phone and I answered and asked her why she was calling Patrick and she said she didn't know that I was that serious about him. I told her yes he was my boyfriend. She said okay and she would never call him again. Saundra was a nail technician so I decided to get my nails done; maybe it would make me feel a little better. I normally treated myself to something when I can afford to, whenever I was feeling sad. It never stopped the pain or fill the emptiness, but it normally eases for a moment.

She was home so I took a cab. I could not wait to get there; my strength was slowly fading, and I was feeling so much pain in my heart that I wished I could pull it right out of my body and destroy it. I could not bear it; I had never been so hurt in my life. The pain was unbearable. I fought to stay strong, but the pain was alive in my heart. The person I was in love with betrayed me.

I finally got to her apartment. I knocked, she opened the door and let me in, I then walked pass her and went straight on her balcony where she had the settings to do nails. I sat down at the table lost in my thoughts until she came and started doing my nails. I could not even put my hands on the table as by then my whole strength was just holding on by a thread; I burst into tears. I could not hold it any longer; I had no choice as my tears started flowing like a river. Saundra asked what happened, I could hardly speak. I gave myself a few seconds before I could say anything. After telling her, she called him immediately and asked how could he have done something like that and let him know that she did not expect that from him.

Later that evening, he came by the apartment to get me. I did not want him near me. I felt like he was the devil. I started trembling, like that fearful child when my mom was about to beat me. As he got closer, I thought of jumping over the balcony, but when I looked over it was too high, and I didn't want to kill myself.

Minutes passed in silence, and he was still there waiting to take me home. I wished if he had not betrayed me, I thought. It was already dark, so I went with him. I wanted to hate him, but I could not. It was like the flames of hell like a magnet that kept pulling me in, the magnet was so strong, and I was so weak. I had nothing to hold on to, so I kept falling back. I felt like if I left him, he would leave with that part of me I could not afford to lose, so I would rather die holding on to it. He gave me life and sucked it back out of me. I just could not let go.

Chapter 13

On my way home, I wished I could go somewhere else to live. I wanted to just get away from facing my cousin and everything. I did not want to go back to live with my grandmother. I would love to go to another country to live but then I could not even leave the country because I did not have a birth certificate much less a passport.

I had a friend who lived in England who wanted to give me a trip. He was a big promoter there. He normally sent for entertainers from Jamaica to perform in England, but over the years, I have been trying to get my birth certificate and was not successful. Each time I went by the birth paper registry department, they told me they could not find it. I had no idea why; guess I was really cursed. Nothing still seemed right; everywhere I turned was a blockage.

Everything was good again, but Patrick started to pick me up at the side of the path where no one could see us. Sometime after my cousin's wife came back home, I decided to move and live on my own. I did not want to be in her space, going in and out anytime I pleased, so I felt like it was time to move.

Outside Herself

At that time my cousin was seeing this girl who had just lost her place and was looking somewhere to live. I told her I was looking somewhere too so we could rent somewhere together. She agreed. A few days after, she called and said she got somewhere, it was a house. She decided to sublet it, so she rented me a room with its own bathroom and closet. I did not have any furniture, but I felt excited to be on my own and it felt like it was time. I went and looked at the place. It was a perfect little room for me in a good neighborhood with the avenues named after the Greek gods; it was even nicer than where I was actually living, and it was not expensive.

I paid for it, got my keys, and cleaned it. I told my cousin's wife that I was moving out on my own, so she gave me sheets, towels, and curtains. I moved out, put up my curtains and threw some sheets on the floor and slept that night. The next day I went and bought a bathroom organizer and a fan. Then I went and bought a bed, one I could afford at the time, along with bathroom and bedroom mats to fix up my little room. It was clean and perfect; it had a closet where I could store things, so nothing was in the way.

The next thing I bought was a Chinese fan décor, something I saw my friend Saundra with. She was good at decorating and having cute things, down to her key rings had to be cute. I think I had adopted that from her. I opened and placed it on the wall over my bed because I did not have a bedhead. This gave the place a vibrant, artistic look. I did not have a refrigerator or stove so the lady told me I could use hers. I was not the cooking type, but I started cooking now and then because it was cheaper, and after smoking weed I would normally want something to eat. I cooked what I was able to. That was when I really started learning to cook. I would ask questions and watch the lady cook sometimes.

Patrick was still around, but then I found out about his main girl. He told me about her when we met; he said he had a girlfriend, but she migrated, and they have a house together but he only goes there occasionally. That was a lie. His girlfriend was still living there but it wasn't the house he showed me. I do not even think the car was his; it was probably hers, but I was not quite sure.

The community I was now living was up the road from his girlfriend. I walked that way one day and saw his car parked but not at the house he had showed me. I talked to him about it, but we did not get deep into it because if she was in his life all this time and he had so much time for me, I could continue to live with it. Somewhere inside I felt like our relationship was not going to last for long anyway now that I was on my own.

I remember one day I was in his car when he said he was going to stop by his girlfriend's workplace to pick up something. I guess now I found out about her and accepted it so he felt comfortable, and I wanted to see what she was like.

She was an auditor at a company. I knew he had good taste in women, so I was not looking for anyone who looked terrible. As we drove on the property, she came out as if she was nearby waiting on him; he went out to meet her. I was still sitting in the car. She was beautiful. She had dark skin, short hair, feminine cut, she was slim and probably in her late twenties.

Outside Herself

She looked like a smart uptown girl.

She could see me from where the car was parked, but it seemed like she knew she was number one, so she did not care who was placed behind her. I did not care either because he spent most of his time with me. It was an accepting moment; it was like at this point we all knew our position. So, I stepped back into my second place with ease after seeing her, thinking I was no competition for her. "My God! I had barely passed one of my subjects."

Weeks passed and I started feeling weird. Something wasn't right; I felt like I was pregnant. I went and bought a pregnancy test kit and found out I was pregnant. There was no way I was going to carry that baby into this world. I already had one I was not there for as a mother should. He hardly saw me. The only time he saw me was around Christmas time and back to school. My grandmother was his mother. My grandmother's two sons were living with her, and her niece, nephews and brother who lived abroad took care of her financially. They were not doing badly, but I wished I could do more for them, so I isolated myself.

When Patrick came by, I told him I was pregnant, and I already made up my mind to abort it. I was not going to tell him, but I needed someone to be there for me. I had no one else and I did not want anyone to know. I remember I had a male friend who lived in Cayman, and he used to send me money for school too, so I called him and asked him for the money. I did not tell him what it was really for; he thought it was for school.

I had called a longtime friend of mine and ask her if she knew any doctor who did abortions and she yes. She had it done before so she gave me the name of the doctor and told me the cost. I liked to have options, so I asked the lady who was living at the house as if I was asking for a friend; she also gave me a number. I called and spoke with the doctor. I felt more comfortable with this doctor although he was way more expensive, but I always thought that if something was more expensive than the other, then it must be the better one.

On the day of my appointment, I was a bit worried and sad even though I had asked my friend about the procedure. She said I was not going to feel anything because they were going to put me to sleep and in no time it would be over. I was afraid they would put me to sleep, and I could not wake up, so it was scary for me. I wished I did not have to do it, but I knew it was the right thing. I knew Patrick was not the right man for me and I was not financially stable, plus I had more reasons not to keep it. So, Patrick came to take me to the doctor's office. On our way, we did not even talk about it. We parked in the parking lot and walked to the office, like a walk in the park, to get rid of a life we made. He did not even say do not do it. That hurt me and gave me more courage to do it. Patrick already had three children that I knew of with three different mothers.

We sat there until my name was called, then we went in together. The doctor gave me an injection and in seconds I passed out. When I woke up, I asked if it was done, and the doctor said yes, and I could lie down for a few more minutes if I wanted to. I lied down for a few seconds and decided I could go home to rest. I took my time and got dressed, then went outside to the secretary and paid the money. She gave me a prescription. I told Patrick to fill it, then I went home to sleep because I was still drowsy. A few months later, the whole process repeated.

One evening Patrick was at my house sleeping when I saw a message from a girl come in on his phone. The name was familiar, and I remember he told me that he met a girl who knew me. I did not think much of it because I did not think he would get involved with her; she was not his standard and she was from the same place I grew up. Her older sister and I were friends.

I was curious so I called her to find out what was going on. I asked her if she was seeing Patrick and her answer was, "Yes, and so what?" I was shocked; I did not expect that answer, especially from someone who I knew. I knew Patrick was a cheater by now but the way she answered shocked me, like she didn't care. I had no idea someone who knew me would answer like that; someone who I would protect in the streets if I saw anything going wrong with her.

I could feel myself getting weak. I was like "Again?" I woke him up and asked him about it, but he denied it. I showed him the text and asked how he could deny that. Based on the message I knew something was going on.

By then tears were forming in my eyes. I did not have the strength to fight so I just started walking out of the house and down the street across the shortcut that led to the main road, where a little shop was that I normally went to buy a drink and cigarette. I did not know I had so much hurt left inside of me for him. This hurt was even worse than the others. I stopped by the shop and bought a pack of cigarettes then continued walking and smoking. Oh how I wished a painkiller could ease the pain. I saw him driving slowly beside me, telling me to come in the car. I felt like he was driving the car over my heart, it was crushed. I was crumbling. Walking was not helping; I didn't have the strength to walk any further and it felt like everything had slowed down. I just wanted to get away from myself. I went in the car and told him to take me to one of my friend's house who lived down the Boulevard. She was living with her boyfriend, and we were all friends.

In no time the pack of cigarettes was done. I used one cigar to light another. I just wanted to die. Everyone there was talking silently; I could see their actions, but I was deafened by pain. What they were doing did not even make sense at the time. I think I went back home after a while, but I was in too much pain to even remember.

Chapter 14

The big man was still in the picture. Sometimes I would tell him I wanted to see him when it was convenient for me, when I felt like I would not see Patrick that particular night or when he broke my heart, and I did not want to see him.

One Saturday, Patrick stopped by me and was in my room as usual when the big man came to drop off some money. I did not know what to do. I really did not want the drama with Patrick, and I did not want the big man to know about Patrick either.

The big man started calling my phone, but it was on silent. He was the type to stay in his vehicle; he had never been in my room even though he was paying for it. I went to the living room and looked through the window and saw his car parked between my gate and the neighbour's. He drove his weekend car, a sports Lexus. Patrick did not know that car, he had only seen the Tundra truck he was driving when they met at my gate previously.

I turned off my phone and told someone to tell the big man I was not there, so he left. Shortly after, Patrick came out and said he was leaving which I wanted him to anyway. My feelings for him were drifting further away. I called the big man long after, when I thought Patrick might have long reached where he was going. I did not want Patrick to come back; I couldn't trust him and things at the time was looking suspicious because I left the room a few times looking outside. The big man answered and said he was at my gate calling and someone told him I wasn't there. I said, "My phone battery died, and I left to borrow a charger. I can't find mine." He asked me what type of phone I was using and said he would stop by soon.

The big man came a few hours later and gave me the money and a charger for my phone, so I ended up with two chargers. I smiled to myself. This man cared for me so much and I was still with Patrick. It was not fair, but how could I get rid of Patrick? I would have to be hiding all my life.

One night, I was in the big man's vehicle at a gas station waiting to get gas when I saw Patrick. I jumped; I was so frightened. The big man looked at me and asked, "Isn't that the car I saw at your gate? Why won't you behave yourself?" I was surprised. I started thinking that all this time he knew I was cheating and still took care of me. I did not answer because I did not want to lie, and he did not say anything else to me, so I kept silent.

That night Patrick called my phone non-stop; I did not answer. I did not know what I could possibly tell him, I knew he was upset by now for calling me and not getting through; it was unlike me. I knew he was going to kill me the next time he saw me, so I just made use of the night in my big man's townhouse, on the third floor, in his master bedroom, on his king-sized bed. It made sense for me to enjoy my last day as I might not have lived to see him again when Patrick finally caught me.

The next day Patrick came. He was mad and I decided I was not going to let him in. I was afraid of him because he hit me before and this time was way more than what he hit me for so I felt like he would kill me. He went around the back and knocked on my window; now he was on fire. I could hear and see the steam coming out of him. I started crying. I locked myself in the room thinking this man was going to kill me. I could not come up with any excuse to tell him; he was a player and knew me too well so he would have known I was lying. Plus, he knew I did not sleep at my house the night before. I was sure he could not sleep so I knew he went to my house looking for me after calling me so many times.

I locked myself in the house until he left or so I thought. I heard a knock on my door long after, so I opened it and there he was, standing right in front of me. He came in when someone was coming through the verandah grill. That was the only way he could come in because he had no keys. He came in, hit me, and left. He was unable to hit me the way he would have liked because other persons were in the house, and he did not want them to call my cousin like what happened before.

After Patrick hit me, I did not see him for a few days. I missed him but this was the opportunity for us to separate so I did not push to call him. One afternoon, I called one of my male

Outside Herself

friends to come over so we could chill and chat. He was happy to come over. I told him to buy some cigarettes for me and red bull to chase the rum I had. My friend came and I went out to open the gate to let him in. As soon as I opened the gate, there was Patrick's car. I was so frightened. Patrick jumped out of his car and grabbed the red bull out of my friend's hand and threw it in the middle of the road. My friend got frightened and jumped in his car and sped off, leaving me alone with this crazy man. Patrick grabbed me and asked what I was doing, then he hit me. I thought this man had moved on; I would have been happy if he did.

The next day my friend called to find out if I was okay and I told him yes. He then went on to say that I needed to leave that man because he was crazy and one day he would hurt me even more. This happened not too long after.

One night, my girlfriend who lived down the Boulevard and I planned to go out somewhere to have some fun. I did not tell Patrick because I told him before that I was going out and within minutes he was at my house. I decided not to tell him. My girlfriend came to my house and sat on the verandah waiting on me to finish getting ready when Patrick came. He stepped pass my friend and came into my home like he was living there, or he was the one paying the rent.

I told him my friend and I were going out and he looked at me in silence as if I should have asked his permission to go. I knew it was going to be a fight that night; I could not let him keep controlling me.

I finished getting ready and placed a little scissors in my purse to kill Patrick that night if he tried anything. Then I went and sat on the verandah with my friend and planned how to get away. Patrick was still in my room, so we decided that we were going to call the cab and lock him in the house. My friend went outside and called the cab, then came back on the verandah. We sat there waiting until we heard a car coming. My friend went out the gate and said it was the cab, so I got up and ran through the grill. I was trying to lock it when Patrick came running out of the house unto the verandah. When I realized I was not getting the padlock to close because of my nervousness I ran to the cab and left the grill open.

The cab driver was someone I knew. He was my cab driver back in the days when Eddie and I were together. He used to tell me how much money I helped him make that day and he would never forget it. He was the taxi driver who took Eddie from Kingston to the airport in Montego Bay and took him back home to Kingston because he didn't get through to leave. Apparently, whatever Eddie charged, he just paid it. He was very grateful and happy.

Patrick ran through the gate and behind the cab. We shouted to the cab driver to drive, the cab driver put the car in reverse (it was a dead-end road) and went down the Avenue. By the time he was finished reversing and to turn the car to go forward, Patrick got to the car and the driver panicked. Although we kept telling him to drive, he did not know what to do because Patrick was holding on to the car by then.

Patrick pulled me out of the car and my friend came out and

the taxi man drove off. Patrick went over to my friend mad and started cursing that she was the one leading me into this. He was so mad. He came to me as if he was going to hit me. He was very rough with me, then I realized I was bleeding. I got a cut on my hand and a piece of flesh was hanging off. I was wondering how this was possible because he did not have a weapon, but I had a pair of scissors.

Everything happened so fast. Then I saw my neighbor trying to get my attention. I had never talked to those neighbours before. He used his hand to ask if I wanted to come in his house. I started to cry and nodded my head indicating yes. He opened his gate, I then ran and went straight on the man's verandah, then he called the police. When Patrick realized what had happened, he went up to where his car was parked and left. He was still mad as I could see him looking over where I was with his face screwing.

I could not tell where my friend went. I then called the big man and told him I wanted to go to the hospital. He asked what happened and I told him I was in a fight with a girl, and I got a bad cut. The cut was bad; I could see the white part under the skin when I lifted it. In no time the big man came and took me to the hospital. I got eleven stitches on my left hand, my dominant hand, so I could not do what I normally would for days.

At this point, I began thinking, what if it was worst. I really needed to get rid of this man from my life. I cannot live like this; this is not me. It did not end there. Days after, he came for us to talk and said his mother wanted to see me, so we went to look for his mother. She and I had a good relationship. She usually fried fish for me, and Patrick would take me to pick it up from her. The bandage was still on my hand, so she asked what happened. I told her that her son caused it, but I did not tell her the story. She nodded her head while she was sharing food for us to eat and asked her son why he could not behave himself. She died years later. May her soul rest in peace.

As time passed, Patrick and I were drifting apart. He was still coming around but not as much, and I was at home most of the time thinking of a way to move forward. I felt like I wasted two years of my life. Now I was stressed out. I wanted to change my life, but how? I started smoking marijuana even harder, like more than once per day, every day. I remember one day I sat outside at my usual spot smoking; I never smoked in the house.

I sat outside thinking to myself that I really did not want to live like this. I wanted to stop smoking and I needed a job. I felt worthless. Deep down inside I felt like I was not living the way I was supposed to. I always thought there was more to life. I admired successful people and wondered how they got there, and I told myself I would never get there because I was cursed. My life did not make sense and I could not even focus or understand in school. So how could I reach anywhere? I could not even see past the spliff tail I was smoking. I could not see any way out.

Chapter 15

The relationship with Patrick had faded. I remember I sent for my son to spend time with me. I wanted to be there for him as how I was supposed to as a mother, but my life was still not growing; I was not ready. I was ready mentally, maybe, but not financially, so I sent him back home.

I started looking for job. I found that they needed a bartender at a bar. What other job could I get anyway without qualifications, so I called, went for an interview, and got the job. I started immediately. After my second week, a man offered me another job. I asked him what kind of job it was. He said he had a business, and he needed a sales representative. I said "Okay, when do you want me to start?" I didn't want to be in anymore bars so I was glad for the opportunity to leave, even though I didn't think I would do well in sales because I never liked to convince someone to buy what they don't want.

I started the job. it was a small business that he and his wife owned selling plastic brooms and a few other little plastic things. The driver would pick me up in the mornings and head out of town to supermarkets and wholesales. I liked the fact that I was going out of town and dressing up, but I didn't last a

Outside Herself

month. I couldn't convince anyone to buy a broom, so they let me go. Maybe if it was dresses, I would have had a better chance.

I called the big man and told him I was looking for a job. He said he was going to call his friend who had an accounting firm. I said okay. He may have thought I had passed all my business subjects, including accounts, but I barely passed English. I didn't remember one thing they taught me in accounts; I couldn't understand it. The only thing I remembered from accounts class was that one evening the teacher was using rooster as an example, saying a rooster don't lay eggs, and I assertively shouted, "Sir, rooster lay eggs!" Everyone burst out laughing. I was a country girl; I heard it said that rooster lay some small eggs.

Anyway, the big man called and said I must meet his friend at his office and bring my qualifications. I told him okay. I scoped up all the evidence of the credentials I had gained, including my nail-tech certificate, as if that had anything to do with accounts.

I got the job, maybe because it was his friend. I dressed up and went to work; they gave me a desk with a computer and put me to work. I didn't know the first thing to do, all I knew was to turn on the computer. I didn't even remember what I learned in the computer course I did years prior.

They gave me printed sheets with information to put in the computer each day. I couldn't wait for evenings to arrive for me to leave. I would sit there, wasting time, watching the clock, and counting down the days to get paid. I knew they weren't going to keep me for long either. So said, so done. I hated it anyway, office job was surely not my thing. I liked to keep moving, not sitting in one place for the entire day. I didn't even collect my credentials. I kept saying that I was going to pick them up until I forgot the address.

Weeks after, Judaz, the model agency manager called and asked if I was currently working. I told him no. He then asked if I could and come work in his bar and grill until he got someone. The bartender did not come to work that day, so he wanted to replace her. I did not mind because I needed a job, and I had a little experienced in that field, so I told him yes I would come. I immediately got ready and went to work. I started working fulltime as I became the replacement.

One day I decided it was time to go back to the birth certificate office to check on it. It had been years and nothing. I called Patrick and asked if he could take me there and he did. As usual, I had to take a number and wait until my number was called, so I sat there patiently. Finally, my number was called, and I went up to the desk with no hope of getting it. I told the lady I had been coming there for years and nothing. I asked what could have possibly gone wrong because I had one before which they gave my mother when I was a baby at the time she registered me.

The lady asked me for my information, while typing in the computer. She then said everything matched except my first name. I asked what she meant, and she said my name is Sahara. I was confused. I asked her if it was Shari and not Sahara, because my alias name is Shari, so I thought maybe they misspelled it. She said no, it was Sahara. She then asked how many copies I needed. I could not wait to get it in my hand to see it for myself.

When I got it, I looked with my eyes wide opened. I was in shock, but I loved it; I really loved my new name. I immediately called my mother and told her what happened. She sounded surprised too. Days later, she called me and said she had it in mind to give me that name but when she told the lady at the registration office, she said that it was the name of a desert, so she changed it. It seemed like the lady put Sahara in the system and put the other name on the birth paper she gave to my mother. I asked my mother if she was sure it wasn't Shari she told them. She said no, it was afterwards that one of my aunts gave me the name Shari. I said okay with a smile; I think I was destined to be named Sahara.

So now I had a new name. I kept telling people my name changed but they kept calling me by my old name. That was what they were used to so I could not blame them. At work, things became hectic; the place started to get busy. I remember telling myself that I should not be working this hard for anyone but myself and I knew deeply that if I put my mind to something, I would give it my all, but I wasn't sure what that would be. I was working there alone until the manager got other people to help during the busy days.

During that time, one of the models who became my friend told me that a guy said he liked me. This guy was a friend of her boyfriend. When I found out who he was, I said no way. I told her she could give him my number, but it was not going to work, but I was always open to meeting new people. He was a half-Chinese guy who I had seen a couple times around my boss, Judaz, named Lee. He was the hottest Chinese guy I had ever seen. I used to admire him; he had muscles that proudly protrude through his t-shirts, and legs that slightly curved outwards at his knees that left a diamond shaped gap in between, and he was always smiling. I never even thought of him liking me. I considered myself not "uptown" enough to get a chance with the likes of him, so I was really surprised when he said he liked me. Or maybe he just wanted to get into pants, I thought.

We started dating and got to know each other. He was pretty cool and not stuck up as I thought; he was down to earth. I remember he bought me a pair of brown slippers with a little heel and sent me to a friend of his who had a logo company to get some shirts to wear to work instead of wearing my normal clothes. It looked way more professional. I started to feel like I was becoming something: an independent young woman who had someone by my side who genuinely cared, and I had stopped smoking marijuana. He had a girlfriend, so I was the one on the side, but he had never made me feel that way.

He started picking me up Friday afternoons to go at this particular outdoor restaurant to have soup, and then he would drop me at the salon to get my hair and nails done. He did not like false hair, so I was wearing my natural hair and he only liked French nails, which I did not mind. I always liked the natural look.

One day, we did not get to go for soup so he told me to take a cab and go to the salon from work and he would meet me there to drop off the money, which he usually did whenever we didn't get to hang out. That day I decided to put some colour on my nails, so I asked the nail tech to put a different colour on each nail. When Lee came to drop off the money, my nails were done, and when he saw the colours he told me not to touch him because they looked nasty. I laughed but I did not change it.

I remember our first Valentine's Day together; he sent me a basket and, later that day, he came and gave me a white gold necklace with a heart pendant. A girl who was working on the property said he was over doing it, but he did not care. He knew I deserved to be loved and that was what he was doing, and I loved him too. Doesn't matter how many times my heart was broken, I was always open to love.

I never saw or called him on weekends. After seeing him on a Friday evening, I would not see him again until Monday. I was a during the week girl; I would go by his house on some weeknights. He had a teenage son who was living with him, but I never met him. He was always in his room when I went in the night and Lee would drop him off early in the morning for school when he was going to work.

When they left, I would make myself breakfast and clean his stove and kettle which always seemed like no one did. Then he would come back for me in the late morning in time for me to go to work.

He started sending me back to school, so I would leave work in the evenings for school and come back to work in the nights after school. It was a lot for me and sometimes I would have Saturday classes when I did not have work.

One Saturday, on my way from school, just as I stepped out of the class, Judaz called me and said that Lee was seeing another girl who was in the model agency who came by there every weekend and he bought her a watch for her Valentine's Day. I believed because Lee always bought me jewelry. I was even wearing a watch he got me for my birthday. I felt so hurt, I got weak. I had planned to take the bus, but I had to take a cab instead. I did not know what to do or where to go or who to talk to because I did not call Lee on the weekends. Occasionally I would see him on Saturdays when his son had some form of practice. He would come into Kingston to take him and maybe spend a few minutes with me. I did not want to go home either because I did not want my sister to see me hurting.

I made my sister come and live with me then, so she could work and go to school. I knew she had the potential to do great because she was doing well in school and there were more opportunities in the city. I wanted to be there for her, I did not want her to end up like me, so I found a summer job working in a clothing store for her when she first came, then after the summer, she started working as a waitress at my workplace and was going to school.

I took the cab and went to my workplace so I could talk to the manager there; she was new there; she was like a friend and easy to talk to. I told her our boss, Judaz, just called me. I then told her what he said, and she said, "What a dirty man. J, don't believe him! Why would he do that? I can't believe he called you and told you that," and that was how I felt better.

I thought I would ask Lee about it. He laughed and denied it; he said it was a lie. I did not believe him because with men anything is possible. I kept wondering why Judaz would tell me that anyway; it did not make sense. He and Lee were friends, and it was not like he rated me that much so I just could not understand. I remember sometime after he told me something about a girl I knew. I could not understand why he did that too because she was so in love with him. She and I were close too, but I could not tell her. It would have crushed her, so I kept silent.

I started looking on the girl's hand when she came to the bar to see if she was wearing a watch. She was not wearing any watch the first time I saw her. As time went by, I was still looking. I think I saw her with a watch once, but it did not look like Lee's taste, although in the back of my head I kept telling myself that it was. I started hating the girl; I could not stand seeing her. She looked so comfortable coming there with her friends laughing and taking my man. I started to wonder why I was even hurting when I knew I was his side chick; I could be dropped at any time.

Now I did not trust Lee anymore. I was not comfortable in the relationship anymore. I just kept going to school. I was still not learning as I should. For some of the things the teacher taught, I was just there taking notes, as usual. I still could not understand why I could not learn like anyone else.

I remember paying the teacher to do my Principles of Business SBA, which would be about sixty per cent of my overall grade. After I did the exams and got the results, I barely passed it. I remember my teacher asked me how I did not get a higher grade and if I could not express myself. I held my head down; I felt bad when he asked but it was my reality. I did not know what was wrong with me, I was just never there in class. *They saw me, but I wasn't there. They saw me on the inside, but I was somewhere on the outside.*

Chapter 16

It was now two years since I had been working at the bar and grill. A group of men who used to hang out somewhere else started coming there. The place they used to hang out was closed down, so they came to my workplace and liked it. It became their hangout spot. They would play dominoes and pool and drink all night; they were good businessmen. They became family.

One early morning, while I was alone at work, a man who had an office in the area came by. He and I were there chatting until a young guy who was down by the car lot, who seemed to be looking for a car to buy, came up to the bar. The property also had a car wash and car mart; all was owned by Judaz. He was standing there as if he was waiting on someone. The man who I was talking to by the bar asked me who the young guy was, and I told him I did not know; probably he came to buy a car or something. The man then left, went next door, spent a few minutes on his phone, then returned and sat where he was sitting before. The young guy was still in the bar area walking and sometimes talking on his phone, and another time he would just be standing there. It was not a big deal to me because people did that all the time.

Outside Herself

Shortly after, I saw a group of police cars coming on the property. The policemen came jumping out of their vehicles like soldiers with guns in their hands and came straight up to the bar. I was wondering what was going on. I had a buzzer to notify them if anything was happening at the bar, but I knew I did not; everything was normal to me. The leader of the squad then asked me if I called the police and I told him no with a puzzled look on my face. He repeated his question louder in a way like he was telling me that I was the one who called them while the other police went over to the guy and searched him. I then said to myself, what if I had actually called the police? Is that how he would have just come and make it known like that? What kind of police was he? The man I was talking to was sitting there as if nothing was happening. They searched the guy and I do not think they found anything on him.

After everyone left, I realized that it was the man who went next door and called the police. I remember he said he saw like the guy had a gun, and then I stared and started to wonder if he and the police were friends, why the policeman came asking me if I was the one who called the police as if he was stating that I was the one who called to protect the man.

Later that day, the men who always came to the bar, the ones who became family, came by. I was surprised they came so early that afternoon. The one who was the closest to me came first, then the others started driving in minutes later, one after the other.

Before they started drinking, two big bikes rode up on the property. One of the guys was the guy who was there earlier who the police searched. He did not ride a bike earlier, he drove a car. I said to myself that this guy came back to hurt me because he thought I was the one who called the police on him. I kind of had an idea how ghetto boys think; I lived there once so I knew they came to kill me, I felt it. I turned and looked before me and realized that every man who sat before me around the counter had a licensed firearm. It was about six or seven of them and it was like they built a wall around me and did not even recognize it. It must have been God who sent them that early to protect me. One of the young guys came up to the bar and walked around as if he was checking out the men. His eyes were mostly on the men; he did not order anything. I was there watching him until he left and went back down and said something to the guy, then they left. He must have seen that the men around me were armed.

I wondered if I should continue working there, but I did. I needed the job in order to survive.

One night, one of the men who I got too closed to took me home and we were sitting in the car at my gate for a few minutes before I saw Lee's car coming up the avenue. I was so frightened, I became glued to the seat in fright. I did not even come out of the car because I did not want him to know I was in it. He had called me earlier and I did not answer because I was planning to call him back as soon as I went inside. He was the type to call sometime to check on where I was. He drove passed the car and then turned around and left. I felt like it was a set up. It was late, and normally he would have been home that hour of the night. I would not be surprised if it was my boss, Judaz; I couldn't trust him. I felt so bad; I felt like if we should break up, it should not be this way. I could not be the one at fault because he was a good man to me.

I said to my friend that this could not be happening. I told him he needed to take me by Lee's house. He asked where he lived, and I told him. He said okay, even though it was far. On my way, I called Lee and he would not answer. When I got to his house, I saw his car in the driveway, so I knew he was home. I went and rang the doorbell for a while. It was a two-story house so it was not like I could go and knock on his window, but he must have heard the doorbell or see me outside because he had a camera at the front. I left feeling hurt and disappointed in myself.

That night I told my friend to let us go to the club, a little music would make me feel better. We ended up at a popular strip club. We stayed there until I got drunk, then he took me back home.

The next day I still did not hear from Lee. He drove pass my workplace and did not even look. I think I had a connection with him or the car because if I was around the back doing something, as I came around to the front, I would see him passing. It did not matter what I was doing, I would always look up in time to see his car. I would smile to myself.

We got back together but the relationship was not that strong anymore. This time, on my birthday, I was sad because I was used to him giving me gifts and I missed him. I missed the days when we were closer. That afternoon I saw him drive in and went straight to the office. I was sitting under a tree watching him; the bar and grill was an outdoor setting. I sat there until I saw him coming up towards me with nothing. I started thinking that the relationship was really over but then he came and gave me a little box and wished me a happy birthday. He remembered; I wasn't really expecting it. It was another watch. He had bought me a silver Guess watch before; this time it was a gold Seiko. I smiled and told him thanks, then he left; I felt happy. I sat there thinking that I had never told anyone how they truly made me feel; I had never told anyone I loved them. I always wanted to, but I was too shy. I could hardly look someone in the eyes. I always just smiled and said thanks.

I continued working there for a while until Judaz got a girl to manage the bar because the other manager had left. I really did not see the potential in this new girl, and I believed I was there long enough to be the manager.

One night I was off, and they asked me if I could work because they had some activity going on and it would be crowded. So, I worked but when it was time for me to get paid, they said they were not paying me for that night. By then I did not feel like I belonged there anymore. I felt my time was up and I was working hard all those years and never felt appreciated. I walked off the job not knowing or even thinking how I was going to survive. My sister was still working there. Deep inside I did not feel wrong; it felt like I did the right thing.

Days after, reality kicked in. I had no money and no job. It doesn't matter how much I worked, it was never enough to save. I think money lost its value as soon as it touched my hands or it just disappeared; every area of my life was just hard.

Outside Herself

I called one of my friends who I met over the years and who was living in Montego Bay. I told him I was coming to stay for a few days because I needed a break. While I was there, I told him that I came to Montego Bay to do scamming. I wanted to learn how to do it; he laughed and said "What?" He said that some guys who did it came around sometimes. I remember I sat there listening to them and asked myself how people really send them money. Some of these persons cannot even speak proper English. Even though I was with them, I could not do it; it did not feel right so I did not even try. I packed my things and went back to Kingston.

I went to a pool bar to have a drink and play pool just to clear my mind. It was up the road from where I used to work. While sitting at the bar, a guy came and asked me if I was not working down the road anymore. I told him no. He then said they needed workers and if I was interested, I could get a job. I told him yes, even though I wanted to leave that environment, but what to do? I took the job; they said I could start in a few days. The guy told everyone that I would start working there in a few days, so I spent the rest of the evening there to get familiar with the place and people.

Chapter 17

A couple weeks after I started working at the new place, I met a man named John. He was visiting from Canada. He came to play pool and we became friends. He would come every evening, sometimes with two guys and other times with one. The guys were working for him; one was his bodyguard and the other was his driver, he said. We would have conversations during my break; he was pretty funny. He made me laugh and it was a joy for him to watch me walking across the pool hall.

One day he said to me, "Let us move to Mandeville" I answered "Really? I'm ready!" He asked if I was serious, and I told him yes. He then said he was currently looking for a place to rent in Mandeville.

On my way in the dark to another parish with another man, Lee called, sounding like he was already in bed, asking where I was. I told him I was on my way to Mandeville. He said okay, and we hang up. Just as I hung up, I remembered it was his birthday. It was a bit heartbreaking; our relationship had ended. He didn't call since I walked off the job. I felt we left the same place we met, so I moved on.

Outside Herself

I was excited to live somewhere else as a stranger. I was the type of girl who if someone called me and said they were going out of town I was ready. Traveling was fun for me. My grandmother used to say a wandering spirit was following me. One moment I would be standing beside her and in no time, I would disappear to miles away. I was always leaving. *I felt like each time I thought I caught up, myself was already gone. I couldn't keep up; I was too slow.*

My new home in Mandeville was really nice; it was a huge two-bedroom condo on the second floor, fully furnished with white furniture, jacuzzi, bath and other things. It was very clean and safe with an electronic gate. I liked it.

I remember going to a vintage car show at the golf club one Sunday evening; I felt like I was in heaven. I loved vintage cars; it brought me so much joy to look at them and hoping I would own one someday.

While living in Mandeville, I was in a town where I knew only John. I was getting a bit bored, so he signed me up at the golf club. Golf was his thing; he played golf every day. He signed me up so I could have access to any activity they had, and he got me a coach to teach me how to play tennis.

One day he came home after golfing and said he found a perfect friend for me. He knew I was bored and had no friends, so there was this spot where he normally stopped to have a beer after golfing. He met a girl who worked there and said we could go by her to have a drink and also so I could see her. I smiled and said okay. I was not really into girlfriends; most of my friends were male but I was open to meet her.

In the evening, we got dressed and went to the bar and grill to have a beer and to meet this girl. She was the bartender there and her name was Dahlia. We chatted and had a few beers, but we did not click at the moment even though she was entertaining. She liked to talk it seemed.

After that, sometimes I would stop by her to have a beer and jerk chicken. One day John invited his brother and his wife to Jamaica. We went all over the place, including the North Coast and Negril for over a week. John then decided to take them to our place for a few days before it was time for them to leave.

One afternoon, we decided to stop by Dahlia's place to have lunch. We all sat at a table eating, then Dahlia joined us. My intuition led me to look under the table and I saw Dahlia using her foot to rub John's foot. I did not want to cause any drama, so I kept my cool.

The next morning, I went to the golf course with John. I told him what I saw. He apologized and asked if I wanted him to stop going there. He continued to say that Dahlia had been calling and asking him for money to buy birthday cake. "Babe, you are the boss. I will do anything you tell me to do," he said. I told him I just did not want to be around her, so we just cut her off.

Weeks after, John and I had an argument about me sleeping too much. I would be sleeping when he was horny, so our relationship was not going to work out. I left and went back to

Outside Herself

Kingston, and he came back for me a few days after. I told him that whenever time I had sex, it hurt so I did not enjoy it. I could not stand when he touched me.

The day he came for me, he told me about a karaoke host that he met, and he wanted me to meet her. That night we went to the karaoke and just as we entered the door, she ran out to meet us. She then looked at me and said, "Damn right I'm gonna like her." Obviously, John had told her about me. We went inside and it was a good karaoke. A lot of people were there; it was like a hotspot in town. We continued to go there almost every week. Even when John was not around, I would go by myself to play pool.

John would go back home to Canada every few months. Sometimes when I was getting grumpy, he would say it was time for him to leave. He would then stock the refrigerator with food and put money on my debit card to pay the bills. One night after John left, Marisa, the karaoke girl, came to me and asked if I could let her friend stay over for the night because she lived far, and it was too late for her to go home. I told her yes since I was there alone, and I would not mind the company. The name of Marisa's friend was Sasha. Sasha stayed that night and never left.

I had started a modeling agency, which was John's idea, because he loved to be around a lot of girls. We would normally recruit girls and invite over a few to keep parties, which ended up being an orgy party, which I didn't mind. I loved watching him being pleased by others while I enjoyed being the host.

Sometime later, after John had returned from one of his visits back home, he shared his idea of me and Marisa partnering in a karaoke business. Karaoke was not my thing, but I agreed. I always wanted to be independent, and he knew that. John always asked me why I can't relax and just be pretty, but I could not do that. I was not comfortable with him being totally responsible for taking care of me. I wanted to do something for myself to generate some money. I always wondered "What if?"

We called Marisa and told her to come over so we could have a meeting. When she came, she smiled and said she left a girl outside in the car because she was afraid to come upstairs. We asked who it was, and she said Dahlia, the bartender. I said "Oh, she can't stay out there in the car. Let her come up." By then I had forgiven her, so she called her in. We then had the meeting had a few drinks and relaxed having chats and laughs. We started the karaoke business. John bought the equipment, and Marisa was responsible for downloading the songs and hosting. We then got a couple gigs around the area.

One day, I took a trip to Kingston when John called me and said, "Babe, guess what? I got a club for you in St. Elizabeth."

I answered "What?"

He said when I got home, I would see. Deep down I knew it could not be a nice place because of his taste. John was just a horny Caucasian man with little or no class. I was sure his bodyguard and driver had put that idea inside his head. So, when the driver took me to see the club, I was not surprised; it was nothing of my class. It was a small strip club, but I went along with it. I went and got it registered and opened the bar. Next, we needed to get the dancers.

We decided to drive around in the parish to recruit dancers and to see how the clubs operated since it was a business that was new to me. We went to a few places; places I had never been. We visited one after the other.

I remember we stopped at this particular club which had kind of an underground feel to it. I stood there looking around, until I saw a girl who seemed to work there sitting in a costume. I went over to her, said hello, and started a conversation with her. I told her I just opened a strip club and needed a few tips on how things should go. She asked what I needed to know but I was not even sure what questions I should ask.

Looking around did not give me the feeling she was making money. I asked her if she made a lot of money there and she said not really. It was just enough to feed her children. I went on to ask her how she made money and she said by selling her body. I continued by asking her for how much. She was getting comfortable, so she started explaining how it worked. She said they had rooms they paid to go in and have sex with men for different prices, depending on the position. I asked her what she meant by the position. She explained that it cost JMD500 for "back shot," JMD400 for her to "sit on it" and JMD300 if she was to lie on her back. Oh! It was the first time I was hearing something like that. She said it so confidently, like it was nothing. In that moment I felt like I was really underground, in a dark place in hell. Her ambition and taste was below the pit; she spoke comfortably about what she was doing for so little money.

I was heartbroken; I started to imagine the kind of men she was sleeping with just to get a few dollars for her children to survive. I was there thinking that my lunch each day cost more than what she was selling herself for. I was heartbroken and blessed at the same time. I wanted to cry. I then went to my driver and told him I was ready to go home.

I continued to wonder how a woman in such a pit could speak so confidently; it pierced my soul. I could not believe that there were people out there going through worse than me. This sent me into deep rumination.

After a while, I had no interest in the club. I went there to check the stock weekly; the driver was the one who took over. He would go somewhere in Westmoreland to buy girls; He said the earlier he went the better girls he would get. He painted a picture as if they lined up, then he paid his money and chose which girls he wanted. He was obviously not reaching early enough because of the kind of girls he brought back. I did not even want to have a conversation with them; I was scared of them. They were heavy and loud. I am sure if they had to say one word to me, I would run.

A few months later, I called the driver to pick me up, but I was not getting an answer. I took a cab and went to see what was going on, but I met an empty club. The driver disappeared with everything, even the car.

I wasn't surprised. Even if I had interest in the club, it would not work; nothing in my life worked forever and I had never received what I wanted.

John told me to look about my passport so we could take a trip somewhere, which I did. It did not take years to get like my birth certificate. I was surprised, it really worked for me that easy.

We decided to take a trip to St. Martin, we were going to meet one his friends who had a yacht docked there, so we planned to stay on it for a few days and a hotel on the last days. I was excited but wished I was going with someone I was in love with. *Why couldn't it be that way?* I thought to myself. Nothing ever went the way I wished it would go for me. Anyway, even though I was excited, in the back of my mind I was thinking something was going to go wrong, I went to the airport thinking that they were going to turn me back. When I finally checked in, and was waiting to get on the plane, I thought, okay, maybe the plane is going to crash, and I was going die. I even thought about my last words that I was going say before taking my last breath.

We went and came back alive and well, and I have been traveling ever since without those thoughts in my mind again.

Chapter 18

Marisa and I were still in the karaoke business. One evening Sasha and I went to a bar that we do karaoke every week to set up. Normally Marisa would meet us at the venue and set up; that was her job as well as to download the songs and Sasha would help her host. Sasha was very talented; she could really sing. I was just the owner and the person who provided transportation to go to the venues. I did not have a clue about this karaoke thing because it was new to me.

When we reached the bar, karaoke had already started. Marisa had moved on and had replaced my karaoke with a karaoke that she was previously working for without telling me. Sasha and I were surprised and disappointed knowing that she could have said something, plus we needed the money. I did not have a clue that she had a problem with anything because she had never discussed anything with me. I thought everything was cool. Sasha and I went back home in disbelief.

I called John and told him what happened and told him I couldn't believe she did that to me. When I felt like I made one step ahead, I fell back. I wouldn't have done that to her; I needed to be like her and stop looking out for people. John said, "Don't stop being kind to people." I thought to myself with tears forming in my eyes that I really couldn't, even if I tried. It was so hard for me to treat people mean. I was the type who would give whoever is around me anything. I would make sure everyone looked good when we were going out. I never wanted them to look or feel any less, so I would even give them my clothes if I had to, even though I never had enough. Everyone in my crew had to look good.

I remember around that time a girl who was with me at my house left to spend time with her boyfriend. In no time she was back; I was surprised. I called her in my room and asked her how she was back so early. She said "Nothing." I told her I knew why. I told her she had an infection. She looked at and asked how I knew. I looked at her and smiled. I had been smelling something familiar on her earlier that day when we were watching television but didn't say anything because I wasn't sure. I immediately called John to send me some money to take her to the doctor, which I did and filled her prescription and gave it to her. Right then I wished I had someone in my life like me.

The following day Sasha and I tried to set up the karaoke by ourselves. We planned to continue with the karaoke because Sasha could be the host. We had an old car that John's security bought; it was the oldest car on the road. I don't know where he found it; it was a Mazda 323 that I called Betsy. He was not a driver, so I took the car. I insured it, then started driving it. I remember seeing a girl I knew showing her friend my car and they laughed at it. I did not say anything to her because I knew it was old and that was my life. I was never lucky enough to get anything my heart desired.

I got a gig in Kingston at the bar and grill where I worked. I started doing karaoke there every week so I would drive my old Betsy to Kingston every day with Sasha and Dahlia. Dahlia had become really close as she was basically living with me, and no one wanted to go home.

One night, John said to me that I needed to get rid of them because he could not even sit and watch television in the mornings before golfing because Dahlia would be on the couch sleeping. I told him okay, and I would tell them in the morning.

The next morning before I even got up, I heard John cursing and yelling, "Get the f*** out of here! Go home and don't come back! I can't even enjoy my own living room." He ran out both Dahlia and Sasha; he was so upset. Dahlia went home, but John called me one night and showed me Sasha sleeping in the washroom. We felt sorry for her and took her back in.

Dahlia, Sasha, and I started going to Kingston every week. John would pack my lunch bag for the road. He was like that; He cooked for me every day: breakfast and dinner. He would ensure I had food, money and he even bought me a bluetooth headset so I could talk on my phone handsfree while driving.

We had fun on the journey to and from Kingston. We would laugh so hard like three big kids; I had a funny side which you would only know if you were around me long enough. Betsy was so old that at one point whoever was sitting at the front would be the indicator on that side. Things hardly worked on Betsy. Sometimes Betsy would not start so I would go under the hood and use a stone to knock something, then it would start working. We loved Betsy; she was everything to us and was always filled with pretty girls.

One evening, I was home alone and decided to go to Kingston. I went to a gas station and put gas in Betsy and asked them to service her. On my way cruising on the toll road, listening to music on my iPod and singing out loud having a good time, the car bonnet flew up and hit the windscreen and broke it. It seemed like they didn't lock it properly at the gas station. I stopped and tried closing it. A truck stopped and the driver came out and helped me, then I continued on my journey. I thought to myself, every time my mind felt at ease, something bad happened.

I was on my way home the next day when I ran into a police officer roadblock. They stopped me. I was wondering why they stopped me. They said my windshield was broke. I said told them it broke the day before. He said they were going to take my license plate. "Omg, like seriously. Betsy is so old and you're doing this? Come on!" I pleaded. I regretted going to Kingston. I didn't have a dollar to go fix it and I didn't want John to know I went to Kingston without telling him. They took the license plate and I had to get the windshield fixed before going back to Kingston to pick it up.

My brother started working with me. He was now the one operating the karaoke while Sasha hosted. Things were a bit rough though as we did not have anywhere to sleep so we had to be sleeping all over the place. We slept at our friends' house and sometimes at cheap motels. I did not want to go by my sister, so we would travel back to Mandeville the following day.

One day, after reaching home, Trevor, the bodyguard, and John were sitting in the living room, so I sat and talked with them a little about my night in Kingston. I then went into my room, but something did not feel right. I shouted, "John, whose underwear is this under the bed?"

He ran to me saying, "Babe, I was going to tell you, but Trevor told me not to."

While Trevor sat there, he then continued saying, "I invited my ex here."

I was surprised to know that she broke his heart so much and he was still going back to her. I remember when I just met him, he told me she called and said she was pregnant. They had broken up, but he wanted to take care of the child. I had no problem with that.

Each time he should meet with her, she found an excuse not to. One day she called and said the baby was born. John was so excited; you could see the joy printed on his face. He then left for Kingston to see the girl and the baby, but she did not answer her phone. The next day when he returned, someone called and said she was lying all this time. So, I was disappointed that he allowed her back into his life. Not only that, but I was missing a few things. I knew that day was not the first time she came there when I was gone to Kingston. I started beating him until he got mad and told me to stop.

This man could not be satisfied. Even though I was not having sex with him—I had penetration with him once in our entire relationship—I got girls to please him and sometimes I would "jerk" him off. I did not love him. He was smart enough to know this, but he made me stick around because I was the only one in his life he could trust and he genuinely liked me.

After a while he started to find girls on his own. He would come to me and say "Babe, I've met this girl. She's cute as button. I'm going to let you meet her." When we realized that the girls felt intimidated after meeting me, I decided to stop meeting them. John would tell me about them because he did not want to feel like he was cheating. I would even know the time they were coming over so I would normally leave to go have a drink and a smoke. I found something to occupy my time until I thought they were finished, or he would normally call to check up on me and let me know that the person left.

Sometimes when I reached home, I could see that he was not pleased; I did not even have to ask. I normally asked him how it was, and he would tell me. When he was not pleased, he would be red, drinking his beer and complaining about whether the girl was just lying there like a log or something. He was so funny; he made me laugh all the time. I would just look at him and laugh. He thought I was the only one who laughed at his jokes; I was the only one who understood him.

John was very entertaining. When we had company over, he

would talk non-stop. He would cook and ensure everyone was okay. Even though he was not a big cook, he was better at making breakfast than dinner. I remember I went on the road, and he called me and said, "Baby, don't eat anything heavy on the road. I'm going to make something special for you."

I said, "Okay, babe."

He would call me to find out how far I was or at what time he could expect me home. He did this so he could know when he should start cooking.

As I entered through the gate and was going up the stairs, I could hear him opening the door for me. He took my bags and said, "Sit around the table, babe. You must be tired and hungry." Then he shared my food and put it in front of me. It was pigtail and cabbage in what looked like a soup. He sat there looking at me, waiting to see the expression on my face. I took my first taste, and it was so salty, but I said, "It is good, baby. Where did you get this recipe?" I did not want to hurt his feelings because he made such an effort to make it for me. I ate some and threw away the rest.

One evening, we invited some girls over. While we were there chatting and drinking beer, he was in the kitchen cooking chicken and steak. He asked everyone to choose the one they wanted. I told them to say chicken because I knew it would taste better. Sasha said she would take steak, maybe because it sounded better. I really do not know why she did. When she got it, not even the sharpest knife in the kitchen could cut it. I laughed so hard.

Sometimes when I was laughing, John would ask what happened because he did not understand the Jamaican creole. I had to translate so he could understand, but sometimes I lied to him because I was actually laughing at him.

I was to pick up John from the airport one day. He sent money for me to rent a car, but I could not get one to rent on such short notice. I went to Kingston, and I got one. It was getting late, so I did not even get to check anything on the car. I just jumped in it and went to pick up Trevor; he was coming to pick up some cash from John then leave. John and I planned to stay at a resort on the north coast.

It was raining a little on our way down. When we were about halfway through the journey, the car slid towards the bank of the road. It was like a little hill, and I did not want the car to hit the bank then turn over, so I swung the car to the other side. I swung too hard, so we ended up down a cow pasture. The airbags flew and the car seemed like it could not stop. Eventually it did and, luckily, we came out without a scratch.

We had to call a wrecker and the owner to pick up the car. We paid the wrecker and sent it to the owner in Kingston, then we took a cab and continued our journey.

John and I weren't together for long. We decided to go our separate ways, so we packed our things and left the condo. We didn't even tell the girls. John went back to Canada, but not for long because he loved Jamaica. I went back to Kingston.

Chapter 19

I moved in with my sister. I took Sasha with me, and Dahlia decided to come also. Dahlia said she could stay with a girlfriend she had met during our trips to Kingston, so I said okay. My ex-boss, Judaz, called asking if I had any girls because a company had an audition going on at his office and he knew I had started a modeling agency. I told him yes and took Sasha and Dahlia to the audition. They auditioned and got the job. I auditioned too but did not get through as usual. I have never been to an audition and got picked so it was not new to me. I had never performed to my ability, plus I think I had passed that stage now.

I went to a sports bar that I usually hang out when I was in Kingston. It was a plaza close to home; my sister and I would go to have soup there on Saturday mornings. The salon where I did my hair and nails was also on that plaza.

The manager of the sports bar was not there anymore so I decided to meet with the owner for the position. I did not want to be a bartender there as I believed I passed that stage and I did not think the place was that upscale for me to be a bartender, so I asked for the manager's position. He said he had it in mind to ask me anyway. We then negotiated the payment. He was not willing to give me the amount I asked for, but I needed a job, so I went along.

I started working as a manager. At first, I did not even know where to begin or what to do. I had worked as a bartender and not a manager, but I did my thing my way. I started to keep my karaoke there every Wednesday. Things were booming; the place was lively, and a lot of people were coming weekly. The vibe was right, but it was not a healthy place for me. I started to drink and smoke every night. I used one cigarette to light another one. I would get high every night with music pumping in my ears and people from all over would come and buy me drinks. I did not refuse because I wanted the place to make money. Being on a high made me socialize better; I felt like I was being myself then: sexy, pretty, and confident. I had an innocent smile and a way of doing things. I was a good flirter, the type who would tell you what you wanted to hear in a sexy, moderate, and teasing way while still keeping it classy. I would then walk away when it was getting hot and leave you wanting more. I never gave too much; I did it for fun because I enjoyed flirting.

At the end of each night, I would put my fingers down my throat because I was always feeling sick, but I would feel a little better after I vomited.

I remember keeping my birthday party for the first time in my life. I had never celebrated anything; I would just get myself a gift when I could afford to but I never had a party before. I grew up in a household that did not celebrate anything or could not afford to. I do not remember any of my childhood birthdays.

I invited a few friends and customers to the party. I provided finger-food and cake and they could buy drinks at the bar. The day before, I rented a car so I could get around and I put Betsy in the shop to be fixed. Betsy was old but she took me many places. A guy who I met on the phone sent me money for my birthday. We met through a man who was the boss' friend and was always at the bar. He had a party and sent the video overseas to his nephew, Jerome; he saw it and said he liked me. That was how we ended up talking. I told him that my birthday was coming up and he sent me money.

Earlier that day, while I was on the road getting things done, I called Dahlia and asked if she could wash Betsy for me because I was taking her to the shop, and she said yes. When I reached home Betsy was still dirty, so I told Dahlia that I thought she was going to wash Betsy and she said she was not obligated to. I said nothing, I was not even mad. I knew she was not obligated to, but she could have said no from the beginning and I would understand because the sun was hot. The mechanic in the area could clean it anyway.

I left and picked up the rental car and did what I had to do, like meet with the chef and other things. There was a lot to get done even though it was a small party, and I had no help.

I remember taking some things to the bar and seeing Dahlia and one of my friends, Theresa, standing upstairs. I felt something heavy came over me. It did not feel right; I could feel they were talking about me. I continued with what I was doing and went back on the road. I had invited a friend who I had met while living in Mandeville; her name was Tanisha; she made her way to Kingston, and I went and picked her up at the bus park. She was pretty, slim and had a nice shape. I liked her; all the girls around were pretty and hot anyways. I picked her up then went to the chef's place. I started feeling the birthday vibe so I decided to call a celebrity and invite him to the party, but he said he would not be able to make it because he had been to the dentist that day.

I went back to the bar to drop off some other things; it was a lot. I was struggling and Dahlia was right there and did not even try to help. That was when I realized that she was upset with me. Luckily, I had Tanisha with me. I said to myself that this girl forgot that we were living in the same room. She had moved out of her friend's house and was living at my place. I was the type of woman who would help the enemy and move on. If I helped someone, it did not mean we were friends. But I guess people don't look at things the way I do.

Night came and people turned out. Music was playing and people were drinking and enjoying themselves. I started to feel nervous because I did not like the crowd, especially when the attention was on me. At one point I went to the top floor to talk to my boss a little; I now wished it was not my party. While there with my boss, I saw the celebrity I had invited, him and a few other celebrities walked in. I was surprised because he told me he could not make it.

I then went downstairs to greet him and were there with them talking in between going to the bar and making orders. I was happy they came; they made my night. I felt like a star, a star that never shines. Even though I had been in the spotlight as a model, doing appearances, fashion shows, music videos and other things, I was not myself. *I was empty, I would curl into myself to feel full, but I was nothing.* So, I was not as successful as I wanted to.

I thought about whether I like the spotlight or not, I was not sure. I felt like a mystery, I wasn't sure about anything. It felt like a jigsaw puzzle inside of me that I was unable to put together. Something was just not right.

At the end of the night, when the party was finished, I felt lonely, and then I realized that I basically did not live anywhere. There was no space for me to sleep on my own bed, so I called a friend and went to his house to sleep.

I started searching for somewhere to live. My plan was to move and leave the others behind. I was confident they could now manage on their own, and I had outgrown that place.

As time went by, I spent most of my time at the bar. A guy started coming there by himself to play pool in the late evenings. He seemed weird but in a good way. He was like a mystery, and I liked it. He was always wearing hats and sometimes a hoodie, as if he was hiding from the outside world and enjoying his own company. He always came alone and played pool by himself. He would challenge himself by making the most difficult shots that seemed impossible to me; it amazed me when he actually made them. I would watch him attentively with a smile as if I was his biggest fan and cheerleader. I started playing with him because he was a good player, and I was always open to learn so I could master myself. We became pool friends; he was fairly intelligent, funny and seemed to be a thug with a soft heart. I started looking forward to seeing him come in every night. I would feel happy when I saw him enter through the door. He never hung around, he would just play a few games then leave.

One night, as he was leaving, I called him and officially introduced myself. I told him my name and that I was the manager. I then asked him why he always seemed to be in a hurry to leave and if he wanted to have a drink with me. He smiled and said okay. By then I already knew his name; his name was Carson. We drank and chatted for a while then we exchanged phone numbers before he left.

We started talking on the phone now and then. One evening, I called him a few times but did not get him. I then sent him a text asking if he was okay. He called sometime after and said it was weird how I sent him a text asking if he was okay, after calling him so many times without being successful. I asked what he meant, and he said whenever a girl called him and did not get through, she would be mad. I told him I had no reason to be mad; sometimes things can happen. Then I realized that we did not even have a conversation about whether he was single or not, but I think sending him that text captured his heart and never left.

After that day, we became closer, and I decided to give it a try. He was just a few years older, and I had been dating way older guys most of my life. He would pick me up every night after work and we would go all over the city at nights after work. We went party-hopping and smoked weed, it was fun being around each other. We would chat and laugh a lot. There wasn't a dull moment around each other.

He liked and shine light on the simple things about me that I wasn't even aware of. Things that I had developed through my shyness that turned out to be cute. He liked the way I played with my hair when I was speaking, my hand gestures, the way I twisted myself effortlessly when posing for a pic; he liked the way I laughed, the way I talked, he liked the way I walked, he liked my boobs, he knew I loved butterflies and everything about me was amazing to him.

I slept at Carson's house every night from we started dating. I was more comfortable at his house, even though he was living with his mother and little sister. I did not see them, so it was not really a bother. The girls were still living at my house. My sister had moved out and I did not even realize. My bed was almost broken down; dirty clothes were all over the place. I did not want to go there, or even bathe there. I found myself throwing clothes in my dirty basket until it was full and running over. I was getting nasty; my little room was not a room anymore.

I remember going there a few times and seeing the picture I had taken not too long ago and had stuck it on my dresser mirror on the floor. Each time I took it up and stick it back on the dresser, it seemed like someone took it down and throw it back on the floor. They walked all over me until it disappeared.

I started losing things. The lady I rented the place from, and everyone started stealing my things. At that time, they were stealing from me at the house and at work. They stole my CPU at work, and I was sure it could only be someone who was working there who did it. They stole my necklace that Lee bought me; that was the first time I took it from around my neck. My life felt like it was falling apart.

Chapter 20

When my CPU went missing at work, I thought it was the previous manager who came there and stole it because he was in graphics, and I could not think of anyone else. I remember telling my little street friend and he asked me what I wanted him to do, so I told him to go burn down his house. He said okay, but then I told him I was just joking and laughed it off.

A bartender was there working long before I started working there. She was a little older than me, her name was Natasha. She started giving me an attitude for no reason. One day I asked her what was up with the attitude, and she said, "It's a woman thing. Women are like that around other women." I refused to believe because I had never given anyone attitude around me. It did not matter how many women were around me, we just did our work and got on with our business. I started to wonder if it was because I was a bit younger than her, and she felt like I should not have been above her. I do not know but I have never given her a reason to behave like that.

One day, she came to me and asked if I could loan her some money to pay her rent. I did not have any money, but she knew

Outside Herself

I had the boss' money. I kept the money each night until the end of each work week when I would meet with him. I told her I was going to loan her out of the boss' money so she should ensure I got it back at such time. I loaned her because I knew how it felt to want something and have no help. The next day she came to work and gave me the money. I said to myself, she did not need the money. She then started giving me an attitude and I could not take it. I did not believe in working or living with people who made me uncomfortable (or vice versa) so I would try to fix the problem.

I called the boss and told him I needed to talk to him about Natasha and he said okay. The boss called us to meet with him. He asked what was happening, and I told him about her attitude. She then said I told the other bartender that I loaned her money. I stood there speechless and confused. I almost believed her. She sounded convincing and I did not believe someone would make that up, so I did not say anything. She said I had told someone something that my boss told me before. I didn't remember; I guess it wasn't even that important to either me or my boss because he never stop telling me anything, so I think she used that as a disadvantage to lie on me. I went back upstairs to the bar and sat there thinking. I did not do that; I was not the type who was going to do someone a favor and talk about it. I had no reason to tell the other bartender anyway; we were not even that close. The only way I could have said anything like that was if she had borrowed money from me and I would maybe tell her that I already loan Natasha what I had, and that should not have been a big deal. I realized this girl lied on me, but why? Anyway, time passed, and the attitude continued now and then. I tried to ignore it because I was not going to stay there all my life.

One night, I overheard her talking to someone about cologne. It was a cologne I loved so much and was missing. I wondered if it was her who stole my cologne and it rested on my mind all night. I was confused; I knew I had been missing things: shoes and clothes, but those were from my house. I always brought my colognes in my bag to work and they kept disappearing.

The next morning, I went to work early to meet with the stock taker and the bartender who was coming on that day. The cologne thing was still on my mind. I said out loud to the stock lady, who was my friend, "I can't believe Natasha would steal my cologne?"

The bartender was new as a worker but not to the area; she heard what I was not hiding. I was the type of person who would admit anything I said about someone if confronted, so if it was a secret, I would keep it until I forgot about it. The bartender called and told Natasha what I said so when Natasha came back to work, she came with her attitude again. I asked her what was wrong now and she said she heard that I said she stole my cologne, and she did not want to beat me. I smiled to myself because people always thought they could beat me.

I sat there looking at her without saying a word and thinking about her wanting to beat me when she was the one doing me wrong. I even wondered how she felt when she lied about me loaning her money, yet she was going in my bag. How degrading was that? I think that was very low; at the time my handbag was my only privacy; I even had a couple of sex toys

Outside Herself

in it that I was hiding from my sister before giving them away. I could have never done that to someone. I never even had the thought of going into someone's bag. Sometimes I even had used underwear that I took off when I slept at Carson's house and forgot to take it out because I was in a rush. Nothing added up when it came to her, so I shook the thoughts out of my head and moved on with my day. I think I ended up firing that bartender; she was no longer working there.

I did not want to fire Natasha for more than one reasons. I knew that that place meant everything to her. She usually said that everyone who came there to work left her right there in a proud way. It was like she wanted to be there, and I could not understand why.

She had become like a family there; she fitted right in. It would be a fight to get her out because she was surrounded by people like her. They did not like me as much as they liked her. I remember talking to a young guy there and he said he did not like me, but after talking to me, he realized I was down to earth. I smiled and asked him why he did not like me, and he said I behaved like I was better than people. So, I asked him why he would think that, and he said because I did not talk up to people. He did not even have a good reason, but it was not new to me.

People always thought that because they did not know me. I hardly had conversations because I was shy and I did not have much to talk about but myself; I knew nothing, so if I did not know you, I was not going to say anything. I may just give a smile and that was it. I was a woman who would sit on a high stool with my long legs crossed, looking like a queen on her throne and looking into my emptiness. *I was just* an *empty shell that looked pretty on the outside with the rumble of the ocean in my head*, confused and trying to figure myself out and the next stage of my life.

Another day, a customer who was a good friend of Natasha asked me for his bill. I summed up everything and gave him the bill, but he was not pleased about the total; he said it should be less. Their bills most time was confusing because they would come and pay a little and sometimes take more, so I was confused. He was maybe right or maybe I was right, I did not know; plus it was not a huge difference. I was not the one who had been serving him; I just added what I saw in the book. Shortly after, I got a text from him saying, "I tell you di gyal a liad." He meant to send it to Natasha but sent it to me by mistake. I did not even say a word to him, but he knew I read it. After that, whenever he saw me, he would ask if I was okay, and I would answer. I did not give him any attitude or anything.

I always considered myself the bigger one. I never treated people bad even when they treated me otherwise. Sometimes I used to think I was stupid when I heard people talking about not speaking to their own relatives for years and not being able to forgive them. It was easy for me to forgive.

One day, I was at home when one of my longtime friends called me and said, "You need to get rid of those girls in the house, especially the darkskin one." There were two darkskin girls there at the time and everyone was in the room. I immediately put the phone on speaker, stood in front of everyone and told my friend to repeat what she said. She repeated, "You need to get rid of the girls in your house. I'm not sure about the brown one but the darkskin one is no good." I stared at Dahlia because I knew it was her; she sat there on her phone as if she did not hear.

I continued talking to my friend. I asked her what happened, and she said she told Theresa some things about me. That was when it came back to my mind. On my birthday I saw them talking and felt the heaviness come over me. I knew her mouth was not hers. I did not have any secret and I didn't normally gossip, so I did not know people's business and I normally had individual girlfriends. It was the first time I was around girls so close and for that long. Dahlia had talked in my presence about my sister before, saying that my sister said I always want her to work in a negative way, but it was not a big deal to me. I just smiled because I wanted my sister to be independent; I did not want her to end up like me. She even told them secrets that she had never told me, but I did not think much of it because they were the same age group and were just spilling their guts to each other.

I thought about what Dahlia could have told Theresa. It was then I remembered that I told them a story about me and Theresa. Back in Mandeville, Theresa was with me for a while. She and I were not even that close, so I do not even remember how we got to her coming to my house. I did not mind her coming because she was pretty, and I used the girls to attract men to the karaoke and it was a time when John was away.

One day Theresa and I were at home and bored. She suggested

that we go to Ocho Rios at a river party that one of her friends was keeping. I said, "Okay, that doesn't sound bad" without even thinking. We did not have a car, so we took about three different rides to get there. I did not realize it was so far; it was miles away.

When we got there, it was dusk, and the party was finished. I knew her friend who kept the party. He owned an apartment complex near to my home in Kingston. He asked her, "What are you doing down here? My family is with me." He was surprised to see her. I was like, "What the hell! What are we going to do? How are we going to get home?" It was night and we did not know anyone down there.

People were heading home, and the party was far from the main road. We would have to get a ride to the main road, then try to get a bus to go to Kingston. I remembered I had just met a man at the karaoke in Mandeville who told me he lived in Ochi. He was in Mandeville at the time when I met him and some friends. They were there for bird shooting season. His name was Chris.

I called him and he remembered me. I told him I was in Ochi and stranded. I asked him if my friend and I could sleep at his place for the night and he said okay. He said he would meet us at a particular gas station, so we asked someone for a ride there.

We stood at the gas station for a while waiting on Chris. Theresa asked me what he was driving so we could look out for him. I did not know so I called and asked. He said he was driving a BMW. Shortly after, we saw a BMW driving into the gas station. Theresa and I looked at each other because we saw this very old BMW coming and we were hoping it was not the one we were expecting. We started laughing and walking towards the car after he called and said he was parked on the pump so we should walk over. We had no choice, plus we were hungry, so we went over. It was a two-door car, so I let Theresa in first so she could sit at the back, then I sat at the front. I put my seat belt on and leaned back and the chair almost broke Theresa's leg. The car was so old that the seat was weak. I said sorry while laughing.

We told Chris that we needed something to eat so he went into the mart at the gas station and came back with two tiny packs of biscuit. We told Chris no, we wanted food because we had not eaten all day, so these little cookies could not do. He said it was late so nowhere was opened at that time of the night. Then he remembered a restaurant he thought might be opened. When we reached at the restaurant, it was a small, dirty-looking place on the side of the road. Theresa and I were scared to eat the food because a few days ago after karaoke, we stopped and bought food at a roadside restaurant. That night we could not sleep; we kept going to the bathroom and ended up at the hospital the next day. They gave us an injection. So, we did not eat the food.

On the way, Chris was telling us about this man who owned a lot of the properties around the place. He was even pointing out some, but we could not see anything because the place was dark. While he was there talking, he saw a man parked on the side of the road talking to someone. Chris then said, "That is the man I'm talking about." Theresa said she wanted to meet him, so Chris reversed and let us out to meet the man. Theresa asked the man for his number, and he gave her, then we continued our journey to Chris' house.

Chapter 21

When we got to Chris' house, the place was dark and just as we reached the door, I heard Chris say we should watch our step. I looked and saw that I almost stepped in a pile of cow poop. Chris lived on a farm it seemed. We went inside, and just as I reached inside, my sinuses started acting up from the smell of the animals and grass. He showed us a room and said Theresa could sleep there and if she heard anything at the window it might be a cow; we laughed. He then said I should come with him so I followed, and he took me to his room where I could sleep beside him. There was a couch near his bed, so I sat there digging my nose and ears. I then got up and went in Theresa's room. We were there talking about how the place smelled and the fact that I would not be able to get any rest because of my sinuses. Theresa said she was going to call the man to come for us and I agreed. So, she called and asked him to come for us. We did not know the address, but the man knew it. He said Chris was his accountant some time ago. He came and picked us up, so we told Chris that we were leaving. He said okay, but he looked disappointed.

We told the man we were hungry, so he took us to a bar and pizza place near to the glistening water; they had boats docked there. We ate, drank, and laughed until it was time to go home. The man took us to his house and showed us our room. It was a nice place. We slept well the night and early that morning the man knocked us up and said the helper was going to make us breakfast and he was going on the road so we should just make ourselves comfortable.

We got up, took a shower, and went downstairs. After having breakfast, we decided to check the place out. It was beautiful; there was a pool and horses. I had my video camera with me, so I started videoing us at the place. It felt like a mini vacation. We ended up spending two more days before going home and then we left for Kingston the following day. We stayed with my sister that day then I left from there and went back home to Mandeville. I left Theresa in Kingston at my sister's house and as time went by, I realized that Theresa was still at my sister's place. After talking to my sister one day, she said Theresa was living there. I did not know Theresa had nowhere to live; my sister thought I was the one who left her there, which I would not do without telling her. She stayed there until she ended up moving out.

I did not ask Dahlia to leave or even what she told Theresa. I also did not ask Theresa what Dahlia had told her. I saw Theresa after, and she talked to me as if nothing happened and I did not say anything to her either.

One afternoon, when I reached work, I remember sitting around the bar counter where the customers sat. Natasha said people talked about me and my management skills all the time and she was always picking up for me. I do not even remember why she told me that because it was not like we were talking about a similar subject and I had just arrived. The persons who were normally talking about me were a man who had businesses on the plaza who I had been supporting long before I started working at the bar, and his friends, who were also her friends and customers. I smiled and said to myself that if they were comfortable talking about me in her presence, then she was one of them. I started feeling disappointed and thinking why they did not talk to me instead of talking about me; they were older businesspeople. I felt like I was in the midst of my enemies at work and at home.

I remember one day the lady who lived in the same house with me, the lady who I rented my room from, came to the bar for the first time since I was working there. She said something pertaining to the girls talking about me daily. She did not get into any details, and I did not entertain the conversation because I knew she was involved as well. I was not the person who liked to gossip about anyone because it did not feel right. I felt like if I gossiped about someone, I was beneath them, so it did not sit right with me. If I talked about someone it was not coming from a place of hate, and at the time I did not have any friends like that to gossip with or about. Carson was my only friend. I slept at his house every night and, most times, left when it was time to go to work. I would just shower at his house, then stop at my house on the way to work to change my clothes, so I was hardly around people.

Around that time, Jerome, who I had met over the phone and

who had sent the money for my birthday, started looking about an American visa for me but I did not get through. I forgot that I had a criminal record which I thought would have automatically cleared but unfortunately it did not.

Sometime after, Jerome's father died so he came to Jamaica for the burial, so finally I met him in person. He was young, cute, and cocky, even though he was physically disabled. He did not have all his fingers and he walked on one of his ankles (from what I could remember). I was surprised because I did not really see it from the picture he sent me. Anyway, I was never going to let him feel bad and I owed it to him to at least be there for him because his father had just died. He was the boss of his crew; he was the one with the money and he had cars of bad boys following him.

I was all over the place with him. I remember being at a party with him and his entourage and I saw Carson; he was so angry. He looked as if he would come and fight me but realized I was surrounded by a group of men. I could hear his sigh in the noisy place through his actions. He then left and I felt hurt for him. I was drifting from him because I had enough of the fun times, and we were not talking about what we wanted. It seemed as if he wanted to live with his mother and pay her bills all his life. I was feeling down and stuck, I needed someone in higher places to lift me up, so I had moved on in my mind.

I started dating a man named Neville, who my friend, Tanya, had dated in the past; she had gotten married and migrated to the States. I had texted her and told her I was dating him, and she did not sound pleased but I wanted to be the one to tell her, so I did. She was not pleased but she got over it soon and we were still friends. Neville had made plans for us to visit the Bahamas.

The day before I traveled, I was at Jerome's hotel. I called a girl to come have sex with him; she was very pretty and sexy. I told him a girl is on her way to come make him have some fun. He went to take a shower and got ready. When the girl arrived, he was already in bed waiting. I told her what to do, then I went outside on the balcony with drinks and cigarettes to kill some time until they were finished. I went back inside when they were through, and I could see on his face that he was pleased and still surprised. I then dropped her off and gave her some money. The next day I flew out to the Bahamas with Neville. Jerome was angry; I guess he missed me.

When I came back, I was replaced; he flew in his Caucasian girlfriend. I did not feel bad because I had a great time in the Bahamas. I was around powerful people who I truly wanted to be around. I was even happy I did not get the visa. I knew at some point I would want to escape because bad boys were not really my thing; well, so I felt. I was still not even sure what I liked. I think I liked powerful men with money, not guns.

I continued dating Neville. Things seemed to be pretty good although I felt a little intimated when I was with him, so I mostly kept quiet. We did not see each other every day; we would go out of town sometimes to meet with clients. I remember on one of our trips to Negril, we made a detour for him to meet my mother. It was her birthday and he had bought a component set for her, so we went and dropped it off.

Outside Herself

I was still looking an apartment, and Neville offered to help. The girls had gone back home. Sasha had gotten pregnant and moved out, but Dahlia hang around and was spending most her time with her new friend. One day I texted her to pack her things and leave. She thought I was jealous, but it wasn't that. I didn't want her around me anymore because I didn't want her to be telling people about my dirty laundry. I met her at the house so she could get her things out. She started to cry; I didn't know my little room meant so much to her. I then remember that she had classes here in Kingston so I told her she could stay. She stayed until her classes finished, then moved back home to Mandeville.

I looked on a few places, but he was not pleased. After weeks of searching, I found one that seemed perfect for me. It was a gated one-bedroom condo with security, fully furnished and painted with earth tone colours which I loved. The furniture was new, including a stainless refrigerator. It was just perfect for a single girl like me. I called Neville and he met me at the place. He liked it too so I told the lady I would take it. The next day I went and signed the contract and gave her two months' rent.

I went home, cleared out some things and packed the few things I had left. Moving made me realize how many things they had stolen from me. I do not think it was the girls; it was the lady I rented the place from; her friend and her son, they had been stealing from me and my sister over the years, but we were not sure. It seemed like they had a key for my room and the girls' careless behavior also gave them access. Everyone was in and out of my room when I was not there. They stole even my savings pan that I was saving coins in, my shoes and everything. Everything I was attached to disappeared. I was left almost naked; they took away the things I loved. I packed the little I had left and gave them to the Salvation Army. I sent my dresser and television to my grandmother's house, and then paid the lady/landlord the difference on my rent for the month. She had my deposit, and since I was there, she had added JM$2000 on the rent, so I gave her the difference of JM$2000. I did not feel like I owed her after what had been going on, but I always wanted to do the right thing.

I moved into my new place. It was comfortable and I felt safe. No one was around; I was in my own space. My sister would come and visit at times.

I felt at peace, even though in the back of my head I did not feel like I was in full control of my life. It was always "What if?" What if anything should happen, how was I going to pay the rent? Worrying was a part of me my whole life. I had no faith; I depended on no one but myself. Even though at times people helped me along the way, I always wanted to make my own money. I never felt comfortable with people taking care of me.

Chapter 22

I went to the doctor for a check up to see if my issue was gone or if it returned. It was so weird when a man saw me back in Mandeville one day on a plaza and said to me that someone was following me. I asked him who it was. He said a short woman. I then said to him that I guess the short woman was not there to harm me. He asked me why I thought I had an infection so often. "Come let me help you." I was surprised he said that. *How did he know that?* I thought to myself. I turned around and looked at him, thinking about letting him help me, but he looked rugged like someone who would rape me, so I said no to myself and continued walking.

When the doctor inserted his finger inside of me, he said, "Feels like you're pregnant." I surprisingly said, "What?" as if I wasn't having unprotected sex and at the same time thinking about how he could know that I was pregnant by just inserting his finger. He made me take a pregnancy test. I was not worried for some reason. I did the test, and it was positive. That was when reality hit. "OMG, I'm pregnant! When did this happen?"

I called Neville after leaving the doctor's office and told him I was pregnant, but he did not seem excited. I was not sure if it was because he was in a meeting or what. His reaction was a bit of a turn off, even though he told me he wanted a child. Getting rid of it did not come to my mind. I felt like I was going to fight for this one no matter what. I actually felt excited. When I got to work that afternoon, I told everyone I was pregnant.

I found out a few days before my birthday and I was still managing the bar, so I decided to celebrate. I called a few friends I had not seen in a while and invited them to my party. I dressed in a cute little dress and heels; I felt pretty and relaxed. It was the beginning of another stage in my life. I had started school again, learning floral and balloon arrangement. My plan was to get out of the bar environment, as always. That night, I told all my friends I was pregnant. I was happy. Something was planted inside of me that gave me joy.

Neville came and picked me up after the party and we went home to continue the celebration. I remember him telling me that I should be careful of those shoes I was wearing that night. I felt like he cared, until months after when things seemed to have changed. I did not see him as often, but he continued to pay the rent and my doctor's appointment; I was barely getting attention.

I started feeling like someone was holding me down in my sleep, which I had experienced before. This shadow man was always running me down to catch me in my dreams. Whenever he caught me, I would try to fight him, but I could not move so I would call on Jesus and that was when he let me go. I have never seen his face.

I had sleepless nights. I felt like a cloud of darkness; a thick shadow of fear came over me. I was afraid to be in the house by myself. I was always afraid, but since I became pregnant, it got worst like when I was younger. In the nights after work, I would sit outside talking to the security until my eyes were shutting down. I was so afraid to go inside the house, but I had no choice so I would go to sleep on the couch with the lights on.

I told Street Boy to come stay at the house with me. He used to hang around the bar. He basically lived there with me, and he was very helpful. He would keep the place clean. He taught me how to cook stew peas and I could send him to the market and just about anywhere. Even though he could not read or write, he would memorize everything and then call me to see if he got them all before he left. I started searching for a school for him, so he could at least learn to spell his name. There was a school I knew of that he could attend, but it seemed like it was closed down, so I did not reach anywhere with it. Sometimes my brother would come by to visit because he did not like it at my grandmother's place where he was living at the time. I could relate to how he felt but whenever Neville was coming over, I would have to let street boy leave, doesn't matter what time of the night and I didn't want to do that to my brother. I did not want him to live with me knowing it was a one-bedroom apartment and I would want my privacy when Neville came.

I was still working and going to school. I liked the course and the fact that I was meeting new people. I met a young girl who

Outside Herself

was drawn to me; she was maybe about nineteen years old. She was kind and used to bring me my favorite mangoes. She lived in St. Thomas, outside of the city. She was very excited about her upcoming birthday, which was about a month away. She said she wanted all of us as girls to go with her to have pizza; pizza was her favorite food. She was adorable and she made me smile over the little things she was amazed by.

After a few weeks, I realized she was missing school, so I asked the teacher to find out why she was absent because I did not have a contact number for her. The teacher called and found out that she was in the hospital. I told the class that we should go look for her because she wanted to celebrate with us for her birthday, which was now days away. We bought things and arranged gift baskets for her, which was also a part of our lessons at school. We went to the hospital on her birthday as a surprise with our goodies. She was in good spirits, happy as always, her beautiful innocent smile lit up the room when she saw us walk in and her family was there by her side. She told us that she had lupus. I was so happy that we went to look for her. I took her number and communicated with her daily. We would talk about food and laugh. She knew I loved stew peas so she said I must call my baby stew peas and we laughed. She could not wait to get out and come back to class.

One early morning, I saw her calling me. I was so excited, thinking she was calling me to let me know she was coming out, but it was not her voice. It was her sister calling to let me know that she did not make it. I could not believe it. In our last conversation, she was in good spirits as if everything was well. I was so sad. I kept in contact with the sister so I could make arrangements for the funeral. Our class made a wreath for her, which was also a part of the lesson.

I rented a car and took my brother and Street Boy with me to her funeral. By then my tummy was big so I did not want to travel that far alone and no one in the class could make it but I felt like I had to go. Her family was happy to see me; they said she was always talking about me. I hated funerals. I would be thinking what if I was the one in the coffin. How would I want to look or whether I would want anyone to see me like that. I wondered if anyone would cry for me and how everyone would leave me in a grave by myself, so I didn't even look on her body. I didn't want to have those weird thoughts when pregnant. I wanted to make a tribute to her. I sat there thinking what to say, I wanted to say something cheerful as her personality. I knew exactly what to say but I overthought it, I wanted it to sound perfect. I didn't want to feel stupid and or maybe I was just not brave enough, so I did not, but I was happy I made it. May her soul rest in peace.

A few months later, I found a letter under my door. I opened it and it was an eviction notice. I was surprised so I called the lady I rented the place from. Her name was Jasmin, and I told her about the letter. She said her daughter was living at the apartment, but she migrated and was now in the process of buying it, but I should not worry about it. I said okay. Weeks later, a man came to the apartment and introduced himself as Mr. Wong. He said he was the owner of the apartment. He was a decent looking man, so I invited him in. I listened to what he had to say because I was renting a place where something did not seem right.

He said he was the owner of the place, and he has not been getting any payment for rent. I told him the rent was paid every month and continued to tell the story. So, the lady fully furnished the apartment, then rented it. Even though she was making a profit for the furniture, she was not giving Mr. Wong his part. He said I could continue to live there but he would not be able to furnish the place. In my head, I was like, "Wow, here we go again. Things just never go the way I want it to go for long." Every time I think things were going right, something goes wrong. I told him okay, and I would stay there until I got somewhere else.

Mr. Wong ended up giving Jasmin notice. She was so mad at me as if I was the one who made it happen to her, but what could I do? I had nothing to do with her dishonesty. I was just a woman who rented the place.

She came and moved out all the furniture, so I was left on the floor. I remember her giving me money from the deposit; it was way less than I expected but I had started a new month, so she deducted some time out of it. She counted out JM$13,000 and stretched her hands to give it to me. I stretched my hand to collect it and immediately pulled back so it would fall on the floor. I did not trust her one bit, so I did not want to have a direct contact with her knowing that I was pregnant. I told Street Boy to pick it up; I never touched it. The next day, Street boy and I went and buy curtains and a bathroom organizer with it.

I had paid down on a queen-sized pillow top mattress before I moved there, while I was looking a place for my own. I went and paid the balance. I dropped the mattress on the floor for me to sleep; my belly was so big I could hardly get up from so low.

I felt like I was on my own. Neville was being late with the rent. He got me a used fridge and stove when it was almost my time to have the baby, which was like months after the woman came and moved out her things. He paid for the bed base I asked someone to make for me, then I paid an upholsterer who I had known over the years to make a one-piece couch for me.

My whole pregnancy felt like years; I could not wait for the baby to come out. I was lonely and stressed. I remember my sister came to visit me at the house and she was there asking if everything was okay, and I burst into tears. I could not hold it. She has never seen me cry, so I guess she told my mother what was going on and she called Neville and cussed him out. I was still working at the bar; I would play dominoes every night. Playing dominoes and having somewhere to go each day was therapy for me.

I would stay there all night sometimes, not because I wanted to, but I did not have anyone to work for me. The bar had a big balcony where people would rent to keep parties and I had to stay there to supervise all night until the party was finished. I would sometimes lie on a piece of couch that was at the back of the bar. I was not even sure Neville knew all these things or even cared, but I had to do what I had to do, plus I only had one karaoke gig at the time.

I worked up until three days before my due date. I checked off the Tuesday and my due date was the Friday. Luckily, my pregnancy did not make me sick. I felt normal and I walked a lot too; I was very active. By then I had changed my plans for my doctor to deliver my baby and registered at the public hospital instead, knowing Neville wasn't there as he should, so I did not want to put myself in any expense. He was still paying my rent and doctor's appointment. I think that was enough for him to do.

On Friday, which was my due date, I got up, got ready and called my cab to take me to the hospital. I did not call Neville. I just told my brother I was going to the hospital. I had let Street Boy go and took my brother in. He was the one operating the karaoke and it was not safe for him to be going down by my grandmother at nights, and Neville was hardly coming around anyway.

Chapter 23

When I arrived at the hospital, I saw a big hall full of pregnant women. I wondered when I was going to get through. I looked around and I did not feel like I belonged there. The only common thing with us women was a big belly. I sat there in my thoughts; no one was even talking to me. I sat there for a little while before I saw a girl who had just rented the bar a few weeks ago to keep her birthday party and she asked what I was doing there, as if it was not obvious that I was pregnant. I told her it was my due date. She asked me my full name and said she was going to call me shortly, which she did.

I went to the doctor, and he asked me if I was having contraction and I said no but it was my due date. He said he was going to send me back home and I told him no. I told the doctor that I lived far, and I came prepared. He said okay, and admitted me. I was happy; all I needed was the baby to be born.

I went on the pregnancy ward, and I saw women crying in pain. I remember hearing this woman saying she was in pain from the day before. I was not feeling any pain and with my first pregnancy I felt nothing. I sat there looking around on what

Outside Herself

was going on with everyone.

After a few minutes, they called me and showed me a bed in a room near the entrance. About four more girls were in that room. I laid there listening to the girls talk. The one who was lying on the bed beside me started talking about her baby's father who had just died and his family who she currently lived with. After listening for a while, I realized I knew who she was talking about. These people lived in the same yard as my grandmother, where I used to live as a teenager. I knew her baby daddy; they were like family. I said to myself, "Wow, *small world.*" I did not say anything to her, I kept my cool. I did not want her to know me, plus my grandmother did not know I was pregnant.

After a few hours, a doctor called me, and I went into the room he was in. He asked me basically the same questions the other doctor asked, then he said he was going to induce labour. I said, "Okay, is it going to hurt?" He said no. He then told me to lay on my back and put my legs up. I got so nervous; I could never get used to a doctor telling me to open my legs. Anyway, in just a few seconds he did what he had to do. I was surprised. He then said I could go to my room.

About an hour after, I started feeling pain. Oh my God! It was the worst pain ever. I could not lie down, sit down or up, stand or nothing. I could not do anything to ease the pain. It happened for less than an hour before I felt like I wanted to use the bathroom. The girls said I could not use the bathroom, it only felt like that way. I was confused. Then I started to feel like the baby was coming. I ran in the labour room and told them the baby was coming but they pretended as if they did not hear me. I jumped up the bed, lay on my back and that was when a nurse told me to close my feet. I had my feet closed for a few seconds, but it did not feel right. I told the nurse that the baby was right there and that was when she ran to me while calling another nurse and delivered my baby. A few seconds after my baby was born, I heard the girl giving birth also.

It was a relief. They took the baby and me to a room on another ward to sleep for the night. I laid there examining all parts of my baby, smiling, and wishing he could talk. It was night and I tried breastfeeding him, but nothing was coming out. I looked around to see if the other mothers were having the same problem; some did.

The next morning, they took us to another ward. I cleaned myself and my baby up. I felt strong enough to go home. I called Neville and told him the baby was born. He was surprised and asked where I was. I told him where and that I was okay. I was waiting to see the doctor, then I would find out if I was going home as one of the nurses had told me. They took us into a room where they taught us what to do and expect with our babies, among other things. Then we were sent back to our beds.

It was almost visiting time, and I wanted to go home. I was not expecting any visitors, so I laid there waiting to see the doctor when I heard my grandmother's voice and two other elders who were living in the yard. I quickly fixed the curtains so they could not see me, because up until then they did not know I was pregnant. I did not want them to find out like this. They came to visit the girl who was two beds away from me. I laid there still, hoping the doctor did not come until they were gone, which is what happened.

After visiting time was over, the doctors came and checked on the mothers and babies. I asked the doctor if I could go home, and he said yes. I registered my baby, called my cab to pick me up and I went straight home.

Neville came to look for us later that day; he did not stay long. He said he just came to find out if we were doing well and how I did not tell him I was going to the hospital. I told him I did not need to, plus I think he would not want to come to that public hospital anyway.

I was happy my baby was finally here. I named him Myles. He brought me so much joy; I missed him when he was asleep. He was everything to me; I got so attached to him. He was my comforter. Neville only came around to drop off money when it was necessary for him to.

Neville called me one morning and told me his ex-wife was going to call, and I should not make things more complicated than they were. Basically, he was saying I should not tell her about the baby. I thought to myself, why would she be calling me if they were getting a divorce? A few minutes later, I saw an unknown number calling and I answered. It was a woman calling to find out what relationship I had with Neville. I told her we were friends, and the conversation was very short. When I hung up, it felt wrong lying about our relationship, knowing it was more than a friend because I had a baby for him.

The lady called back the next day. She was telling me how long they met and everything that was going on with them. It was then I realized he met her when I was pregnant. I immediately told her I had a baby for him, and she was surprised. We continued the conversation about him and the type of person he was and what he was doing to and for the both of us. He had flown out that same day for a few days. I was so hurt and stressed out by his lies. All along he was partially living with another woman and bought a Range Rover that they were driving all over the place, even down by my workplace to meet with a guy who I had connected him to, and here I was having his child. I did not know what I got myself into. I started blaming myself for getting involved with him in the first place, but when I looked at my baby, I had no regrets, and he gave me the strength to try coping.

When Neville came back, he came by the apartment trying to tell me a story about how the girl was just a celebrity's ex-wife, as if she did not mean anything to him. I knew this celebrity; I even happen to be in a studio where he was and ended up doing an intro for one of his songs. I knew he already told her I was just a friend of a friend he used to date. He came there wanting to have sex with me. It was about four months after I gave birth. I was scared to have sex and certainly not with him; I had no love for him.

Neville did not want to pay the rent anymore. The girl and I were still talking, and I remember she said, "He's a dirty man and don't be surprised if you find someone to take care of your baby." It was easy for her to say, no man wanted a woman with a young baby; that was impossible. She had a four-year-old son at the time.

I was swimming in stress. I had to quit my job, I had no one to take care of me and my baby. I did not know what to do. Nothing was ever right in my life. I made poor decisions even when I tried to be careful or just tried to be myself.

Now the landlord wanted me out. He told me he needed the place, and he would give me a month's rent when I found a place. I could not see a way out. I was cornered and could not see or move. I started to smoke again and by then I lost all the weight I had on; I was going crazy. I started to have nightmares about the house. One night, I dreamt that a guy who used to live in the house came and was so mad that I was in it, and he wanted me out.

I was going through so much pain and stress that I could not bear it on my own. One day, I was watching the television and I saw a church advertising their phone number for counseling. I wrote down the number and went for counseling. I talked to a lady, and she asked me what was going on. She asked me a few more questions and then that was it. I felt like it was a waste of time. She did not even pray for me.

Dahlia called me telling me she saw Carson at a party the night before with a girl and they seemed happy. I knew the devil was in her. That was the last thing I wanted to hear. I started to feel like it was karma. Maybe I should have settled with him. I felt like I was my own enemy, like I was climbing a mountain stepping on my own head.

Weeks after, Dahlia came and looked for me and the baby. Then called me days after and told me what she told me about Carson was a lie. I guess she saw what I was going through. She said, "Why don't you start doing something for yourself because this man thing not working out for you." I smiled with a frown. I smiled because of her courage to say that, and I frowned because she had taken the few years she knew me to judge my whole life; she didn't know that I was not normal.

There was this program on television that I watched whenever I saw it on. There were people giving testimonies about how this spiritual man helped them and how their life got better since they visited him. I said to myself that I needed to see this man because I was really cursed; something was definitely wrong with me.

John was still visiting Jamaica and had left his car with me because he was flying out. He said I could use it until he was back. I always remained friends with my exes. Lee was the one who bought me a little "pully" that I packed my things in for the hospital.

I saw on the television that the miracle man would be in Kingston to heal people the following Sunday, which was about two days coming. I told my brother that we should go. On Sunday morning, we all got dressed and went. When we got there, there were two tents: one open tent that people sat under waiting to go in and the covered tent where the miracle man is.

We went under the tent and had a seat. A lot of people were there so the tent was full and people were all over on the property waiting. They gave me a seat because I had the baby and my brother had to stand. I sat there for a while, then I started to look around and all I could see was pain, poverty, and darkness. The people did not look like us; we were the only bright-looking ones there, so I started to feel like I did not belong here.

How bad was my life? I did not look like the others but what had been going on with me my whole life did not feel right; something was definitely wrong with me. Maybe their lives were worse than mine, but how much worse could it get? I had so many dreams and desires, and I could not meet them.

I left from under the tent, walked towards the gate and sat there. Then I heard a man coming down the road, shouting that the man was a false prophet. That was when I said to my brother "Let's go home." I went home, cooked and we ate.

 hapter 24

Later that evening, my brother left for work, and I was home alone with my baby, thinking how my life was ever going to get better. I felt like I was in a grave and everywhere I turned I was blocked by concrete walls with not even a crack in it for me to escape. I could not see a way out. I was about to lose my mind; I had no hope and no faith. My whole life was just a mess from the beginning. Maybe I really should have died because I served no purpose. I was so stupid, I never made the right decisions, and I couldn't even focus or learn. I felt like I was deprived from life.

I asked God, "Why are You doing this to me? I'm a good person with a good heart all my life, and this is what You allow to happen to me." In my stress, I remember a friend of mine called in pain saying she needed to borrow some money to see the doctor. I had US$40 in my purse, and I gave it to her without expecting it back. I always felt like I have to help others. I couldn't have something and lied that I don't have it. Then I realized that I never had enough but I was always the lender or the giver; that doesn't even make sense.

I started to scream. I think it was the first time I ever screamed.

I fell on my knees and told God, "I want to be on the right path. I want to do the right things. Lead and I will follow," then I sat and cried continuously for a while. I was so weak. I went to lie down beside my baby, wiping my tears. I put my finger inside his tiny little hand, and he squeezed it, which he always did. As a matter of fact, every baby does that, but that squeeze felt different; it felt like he was saying, everything was going to be okay. I looked at him and smiled, then stayed beside him feeling at peace.

I started hunting for a house to rent. Every Sunday I would buy the newspaper to search. I also went to several places to look. I would leave Myles with my brother and take a cab or sometimes I would ask friends to take me. I did not go back for Betsy from the garage and by then it needed to be licensed and insured and I didn't have the money. It took me weeks to find a place that I liked. I told the lady who showed me the place that I wanted it. I had some money that Neville had given me for rent so I went in my account and withdrew the little I had. I then went to the place and called Mr. Wong to meet me there so he could give me the month's rent he promised. When Mr. Wong came, I met him outside the gate. He looked at me and said, "Sahara, will you be able to pay for this place?"

I looked at him and said, "Mr. Wong, I'm not going to leave your nice place and go live in a rat hole with my baby. I'll find a way."

It was the first time I had ever said something so confidently that I could remember. It was a two-bedroom apartment, remote gate, no security, but it was safe and clean. I took the two bedrooms so my brother could have his own room; he needed to step up his game to pay his part of the rent.

The lady who owned the place asked me for a letter proving where I worked, so I called Neville and told him. He called his office and had them prepare a job letter for me.

I moved in and was getting settled, not knowing where the next month's rent was coming from, but for some reason I was not that stressed.

We still had the one-night karaoke that my brother was working. That money was used to buy food for the week, although it was not even much. I don't even know how it lasted. I would cook in the evenings so my brother could eat before he went to work, and I would normally leave some out on the stove so he could eat when he came home in the late hours of the night.

Neville would drop off a few things for Myles. Myles was still breastfeeding. I could not get him off my breast, but I would try and feed him with other baby food in between. I was enjoying my baby so much; I did not miss anything. I saw his first roll, his first crawl, his first laugh, his first step, and he started walking pretty early, at nine months. I remember his first laugh was on my birthday, that day he laughed so hard and long that made me laugh too. I told a friend about it, and she said it was my birthday gift from him, and I believed so.

One morning, I decided to put data on my phone to see what the outside world was going on with. Putting data on my phone

Outside Herself

felt like luxury at the time. I strolled through and then continued with my usual day's work. After watching the news, I would maybe watch something else before going to bed. I did not have a choice; I had only one local channel to watch, the others were not picking up.

That same night my baby fell asleep while I was watching the news, so I put him on the bed, and I went to sit in the living room to watch television until the news was finished. I decided to go to bed early that night because nothing interesting was on the television. I went to bed, even though I was not sleepy.

I laid there and got a message from someone on messenger saying "Hi." I replied with "Hi." I was longing to talk to someone and now since I was feeling a little relaxed, I didn't mind. We started a conversation for a few minutes then he asked me for my number so he could call instead of text. I gave him my number and he called immediately. I realized he had an accent, so I asked, "Are you Jamaican?"

He answered, "No."

Then I said, "But I saw Jamaican on your status. Why is that so?"

He said he did not know. I was confused. I started to think, "OMG, this man is a fake. I don't trust him. He's a liar." I started to check on the conversation that we were having and realized that we had been talking over the years. I remembered him but his username had changed. He would invite me to where he lived but he was not a charmer, so I did not give him much attention.

Anyway, I did not really let it get to my head; it was just a conversation, and I was bored. It had been a while since we had a conversation so I continued and told him to take the Jamaica off his profile, which he did.

The next morning, he texted me, "Good morning" but I did not get to answer because I had no minutes, and my data was up. The evening, after he got home from work, he called me and asked if I did not see that he texted me. I told him yes, but I did not have any minutes to reply. He said okay, and he was going to send me some minutes. He hung up and shortly after I received the minutes.

We started talking every day when he got home from work. One evening, it was getting late, and Neville was supposed to drop off some diapers, but he did not. I was calling him and was not getting an answer, so I was upset. The man called, and I tried not to sound angry. I was so used to keeping my pain inside and putting the best outside that if anything bad happened to me, I would still smile. I had never given anyone an attitude based on how I felt inside. No one would ever know how I really felt. I was a pro at that but somehow this man asked, "What happened? You don't sound like yourself today."

I sighed while he was there waiting on me to tell him. I said, "Myle's father was supposed to drop off his diapers and I don't see him and I'm not getting through to him on his phone. He might drop it off tomorrow, but I need it tonight."

He then said, "Don't worry about him. From now on I will take care of you and your baby."

I did not even answer; I was speechless for a few seconds before switching the conversation.

The next morning, I told my brother that this man was talking foolishness in my ears; I even called my mother and told her. A few days later, the man called me asking how much my bills for the month were, including my rent. I told him it was just the light and the rent because the water was included in the rent. He said okay, and sent the money. He told me to get the cable and internet and he would pay for them. I could not believe it. I was so stressed for months, and all my bills were now being paid just like that; it was surreal. I knew it was God, plus he told me he was a church man.

We kept talking every day, getting to know each other. He said I should come to the Bahamas to visit but I told him he had to come to Jamaica first. He said, "No problem" and he did not waste any time. He told me to go online and find a place on the west coast where he could stay. He had been to Jamaica years before and was familiar with that side, the tourist area. He then sent me money to rent a car and buy things for Myles. I asked my mother to keep him for the few days I would be away. I remember when I went by my mom to drop off Myles, she asked me if I was not scared and I said, "No, he has never given me any reason to be." I left my baby for the first time, for more than a day. I missed him but I was happy to be going somewhere.

I reached Montego Bay Airport early because I did not want him to be waiting. I reached too early because his flight was delayed, so I went to look for my soldier friend who was on duty to kill time. After I saw my friend, I went back to the airport to pick up the man. It was late evening, and I could see him smiling from far walking towards the car. I called my mother and let her know that I picked him up; I had been in contact with her the whole time.

It was almost night, so we drove from Montego Bay straight to Negril. I did not realize it was that far. When we finally got there, we were tired. He did not really like the place, but I did not see a problem with. It was not a five-star hotel, but it was okay. Anyway, it was too late to find somewhere else, so we stayed that night. The following morning, we went and had breakfast, then went on the road. I remember while I was driving, he put his hand on my leg as if he knew me for a while. It felt a little awkward and I did not normally like people touching me, but I guess he was just comfortable around me to do that. We drove to Savanna-la-mar because he wanted to take me shopping but I did not see anything I liked there. We spent most of that day driving up and down, then went back to the hotel. We decided to find a place in Montego Bay which was nearer to the airport, so he booked Sandals Royal.

We stayed at the resort for the next two nights, then we went across the road where he bought me two nice dresses. I wore one that night for a reservation dinner and took pictures. We had a great time. He only spent three nights. I went for my baby and went back home the next day.

Chapter 25

I went to Bahamas the next month to visit him. I left Myles with my mom. It was not my first time in the Bahamas. I got there late evening and I was starving. He asked me what I wanted to eat, and I told him I was not sure, he should just take me somewhere. He took me to a kind of local fast-food joint. He said I could stay in the car if I wanted so I did. He parked the car where I could see what was going on. I sat there watching him in the line and I tried to remember if I had ever seen any of the guys I was in a relationship with in a line before. It was unusual for me, but it was something I appreciated.

He finally came with the food, and I opened the box immediately. I was really hungry, and I did not know what to expect. When I opened it, it looked like KFC popcorn chicken. The only difference was, they were joined together. I asked him what it was, and he said it was cracked conch. I did not like conch because I had it back home before in soup. It had a rubbery texture and was almost tasteless, so I did not care for it much. Then I realized they put ketchup all over the fries, so I asked, "Why did they put ketchup on my food? Shouldn't it be my choice?" He said that was how they did it there. I did not like it, but I ate it because I was hungry.

He wanted me to come church with him, so we went shopping for church dresses. It took me a while to find a dress I liked, as usual, but after I visited a few stores, I finally found two I liked. He picked one for me, one that had two different shades of pink with a cut showing my cleavage. I did not feel comfortable wearing it to church but it was his place so he would know if it was appropriate, so I went along with it.

On Sunday morning, we got ready for church. Church started at 9:30am. It was a small church; he went straight up to the second row at the end, in the middle of the church. I felt strange. I was in a different country and at a place I would not normally be on a Sunday morning. My eyes were everywhere. Because it was a small church, there was not much to look at and the people around me were close. Inside the church was not daylight bright; it was cool and had a shade of dimmed light with air conditioning. It was very cozy and comfy.

Church started, so everyone stood up and sang along with the choir. The choir was on the pulpit and a group of young people were dancing to the music on the floor below the choir. Before the audience and beside the pulpit on one side was a band playing music. On the other side was where the choir sat. Everyone was so engaged and passionately doing their part. The choir was singing from the heart, it showed in their action. The dancers were dancing like they were on fire, to the rhythm of the drums that were piercing my soul. Everything felt alive. The audience danced and some were holding up their hands and looked lost in the atmosphere. Everyone was into whatever they were doing and even my man was rocking. I was surprised because I remember asking him for a dance at the hotel and he refused.

Then I saw a man and a woman escorted in; I assumed they were in charge. I stared at them, and the woman looked like a woman I knew back home. I could not figure out their age. The man had a bald spot that made him look old. I was kind of puzzled. After the praise and worship session, the moderator asked first timers to stand so they could welcome us. I stood up and they gave me a card to fill out with my information and suggestions about the church, which I did.

Offering time came and I saw Stephen put $100 in a tithe envelope. I was surprised. I started to calculate the money in JMD; I did not know people gave that much in church, which was like more than JM$10,000. It was time for the pastor to preach. I saw a woman go and put the pastor's iPod and a glass of water on the transparent table, and then everyone stood to their feet in honor of him as if he was a king of the little kingdom. He started preaching. I sat there listening to every word coming out of his mouth. I wanted to have a clear understanding of what he was saying, although sometimes I was thrown off by the accent.

The pastor was preaching like no other; he gave me chills which I never felt at any other church I had been, even though it was a while since I visited a church. Every word coming out of his mouth made sense, I could somewhat relate. He was not just telling an old story from the Bible, he was basically preaching in a way that our generation could understand.

Outside Herself

On our way home, I told Stephen how I felt about church; I really liked that church. He said that was how he felt the first time he went there and still felt that way, so he continued. I remember someone from the church called me a few days later to ask me about the service and how was my visit. I told her I loved the pastor. Stephen asked why I said that, and I asked him what he meant. I was not even thinking any other way than loving the pastor as a man preaching the word with a vibe. I started to think about what I wanted to say before I spoke because I did not want anyone to put a different meaning to what I said. It was a different country and culture so maybe their words had different meanings, which I normally got confused with sometimes when we were conversing.

I was counting down the days to go back home to my baby. I missed him so much and could not wait to see him. I would call my mom every day to check up on him and she would send me pictures.

Before it was time to go home, after spending about a month, Stephen proposed to me. It was not a surprise because he had been hinting me from we met. The ring was so beautiful I could not take my eyes off it; it was my first time wearing real diamonds on my finger. I was not excited to get married, even though I thought about getting married someday. I always told myself that I was only going to marry once in my lifetime. I was not even sure he was the one because we had nothing in common and we hardly knew each other. I was not even in love with him. I wanted to marry someone who I was crazy in love with, but then I accepted that things just would never go my way. He made me the one, so I went along.

When I got home to my baby, it was night. I remember I stretched my hands out to take him and he turned away because he did not recognize me. He got attached to my mother for the weeks I was away. It was the next day before he realized that I was his mommy and everything went back to normal. We left two days after and went back home.

Stephen continued to call us every day to checkup as if we were the only ones in his life. He made sure we were not short of anything, and he would ask for pictures of me and Myles daily. Stephen did not waste any time as usual; He told me to look about Myles passport so we could come home.

He came two months after and that was when he officially met my mother and Myles. The three of us spent the Christmas at a resort and left for Bahamas after the holidays. We got married a few months after. I watched him as he slowly put on diamonds while saying his vows on the hand that had a scar caused by another man. We did not have a big wedding, just had two witnesses, one was his friend and his friend's ex. Stephen did not have any friends. He said everyone left when he got saved because he did not have any more rum around him for them to drink.

After we got married, we just went to pick up Myles at a daycare and preschool that we dropped him off until we were finished. We did not even go for lunch. Everything was new to me; I did not even know what to do. I started to think about why we did not have a wedding. I felt like I never made enough effort in getting things done the way I wanted but that was maybe because I never knew what I wanted. I was always stuck

Outside Herself

between positive and negative thoughts. Then I started blaming Stephen that he was the one why we did not have a wedding. It was not a big deal for him because he was married twice before, so I think his experiences took away mine.

Living in the Bahamas, married and going to church every Sunday and Wednesday night made me feel like I was trapped in a little box; my life was so boring. I was homesick; this life did not feel right but I held on because of my baby. I didn't want to take away the father he knew from him. Stephen was a great father to him; Myles was never short of anything. He treated Myles as his own and he gave Myles the best.

Myles continued the preschool, so I was home alone during the days doing my house duties, with my mind all over the place, thinking about my life and what I wanted. I was never seeing myself as a woman who stayed home taking care of kids and a husband. I was not relaxed but I still did it with love.

I would prepare hot meals for my husband to eat when he came home. I also ensured he came home to a clean house; he deserved it because he worked hard to take care of us. But I would feel miserable at times. I had no friends or family there, no car and he didn't want me to work outside the house. He said he didn't want his wife to work for anyone. I felt stuck and useless. He used to come home during breaks from work and I thought he just came home to watch me. Sometimes he would just sit there following me with his eyes as if someone was looking through them on me. His eyes would move everywhere I went, and his head did not even turn. I asked him a few times why he was looking at me and he would say he was not. It was so weird.

Stephen was the one who dropped off and picked up Myles. I wanted to be the one whose face he saw after long hours at school, and I wanted to be the one to kiss him goodbye. All I had was him, now I felt like Stephen had taken him over.

At one point I felt so depressed and sad; I longed to go out with someone who spoke my language and laughed loudly. I told Stephen that I wanted to go hang out a little with this Jamaican girl I met through a mutual friend, and he said no because he did not want his wife to hang out at any bar. At that point I felt like marriage was definitely not for me. I hated him; he disgusted me. Did he not understand that this whole life was new to me: marriage, lifestyle, country, motherhood, everything, and I was depressed? How could he say that? Was this because he was a Christian? Well then, no, this Christian thing was not going to work. It was not supposed to feel like this; I felt trapped more than ever. There was no way I was going to be a Christian and there was no way he was supposed to be my husband. Nothing felt right.

I remember whenever I said something to him, I would have to kept repeating myself. It felt like my voice was slowly disappearing. I was speaking so low, he couldn't hear me, but I could hear myself so when I spoke up, it sounded like I was shouting in my own ears.

One Sunday, on our way to church, he said he was going to open a church and I was like, "What? I don't want to be no pastor's wife." He said he was not called to be a pastor, he was just going to build one and get pastors to preach, so I replied "Okay." The only place we went to was church. I felt like I was obligated to go to church. I could see the disappointment on his face whenever I told him I was not going. This always led to us ignoring each other for the rest of the day. I just wanted to punish him because he would not allow me to go other places apart from church, which I could go, but I had no one to keep Myles, so I kept my cool.

His "holiness" was starving me from the lifestyle I knew. He would even pray for me when I had headaches. I remember the first time I had a headache around him, and he said, "Let me pray for it."

I replied, "Why do you have to pray for my headache when I can just go take a pill?"

Anyway, he prayed, and the pain went, so whenever I was having a headache and he was around I told him to pray for me. Stephen was always a praying man; he prayed every morning. He never prayed with me, but he prayed for me. I used to wonder what he prayed about that long every day. My prayers were always short, and I only had one prayer apart from the prayer my mother taught me when I was child to say before bed. My whole life, my prayer was, "God, give me knowledge, wisdom and understanding. Amen," because that was my main challenge in life. I started adding, "and break the curse from around me."

Shortly after, I found out I was pregnant. I did not even know when this happened. It happened so fast, and I was not ready;

I did not see myself with another child. I was too scared. What if Stephen died? I was going to be alone with two babies. This could not be happening to me.

I found out later that it was not just one but two: identical twin girls. By then I had accepted that I was bringing two more lives into this world, which I did not hope or plan for but here they were. Stephen seemed to be getting on my nerves and Myles was too hyperactive, and even the house seemed too small. I never felt the same way I did when I found out I was pregnant with Myles. It felt good being pregnant with identical twin girls, and being married, having someone by my side, but I wasn't happy.

I was also stressed out about Myles not talking. I was wondering what was wrong with him. I remember I was talking to a girl at church, and she said he should have been talking already. It just sent me into a deeper depression. Every day I was on Google researching all the possibilities of why he was not talking.

I went to visit my doctor as appointed and he sent me to do an ultrasound. I figured something was wrong because I had already done one not too long ago; that was how I found out I was pregnant with twin girls. The doctor told me to call my husband and we both met with him. He told us the babies were not alive. I was about six months pregnant. I could see my husband's face full of sadness hidden behind a mask of masculinity. I was sad at first, but I think God knows best.

Stephen wanted a child, but I kept telling him no. Myles was his so what more could he want. I tried convincing him by telling him it was time to relax at his age and stop thinking about kids. All his life he had been raising children so he could stop now and just focus on our dreams. Children were so expensive. He took it off his mind years later because he believed he was getting too old to be running down babies.

Some Sundays I did not feel like I wanted to go to church. I did not see the reason why I should go every week. I was not "feeling God." I just sat there listening to the word. I had no passion for God like the people in church. I would watch them surrendering, trembling on the ground, dancing, and agreeing to what the pastor said. But I kept reminding myself about my prayer and promise to God when I did not feel like going until it became a habit. I got comfortable going, even when my husband was not. Sometimes my husband would make me angry and I decided not to go thinking I was spiting him, but then I would just come to my senses and realize I was not going for him, I was going for God.

I got baptized sometime after. It wasn't my first time getting baptized; I got baptized when I was thirteen, not because I wanted to but because I wanted to fit in. It did not look right to me knowing I was going to the church for a while. My husband was a Christian and I was not feeling like I was a part of it. I never felt like I was a part of anything anyway.

I would sit in church every week like I was all that, with my long legs crossed in my beautiful dresses, watching, and looking all over the place and not feeling connected. I sometimes wondered if this was it. I thought some of the people were pretending. I remember one evening at church it was greeting time and we all stood up greeting and hugging each other. I was going to greet the pastor's wife's armor bearer and she looked straight in my eyes and turned her back. I wondered why, then I realized people in the church were just like people on the outside. I confronted her weeks after when they appointed her to preach. It did not feel right to me, knowing she did that to me and was going on a pulpit to preach to people. I did not think that was of God. Anyway, she apologized, and I let her go. I think she did it because she heard my accent. I had seen her a few times at the mall, and she was the one who waved to me. One Sunday, I went to the bathroom, and she was there alone so I politely told her good morning and asked her if she had a wonderful Christmas. That was the first time she heard me speak. I have heard on more than one occasion that they do not like Jamaicans, so that was in the back of my head. I knew that some Jamaicans could behave badly, but I promised to keep my head high because I was a proud Jamaican, and I was not going to be the one to let them look down on my people.

One Sunday, the pastor's wife was preaching. She was also a pastor of the church. She started saying something about red bottom shoes. I sat there listening and saying to myself, I hope she did not think I liked her shoes for me. I liked them for her; leaders must look the part. I told her I liked her shoes more than once. The last time I did that was when I wanted to congratulate her about something that was being celebrated on that particular Sunday. She was nearby, so I stood waiting until she finished greeting her mother-in-law when she hugged her again. At that point I wanted to leave because I thought she hugged her mother-in-law again to avoid me, but my body froze. When she finally came to me, I forgot what I was going to say, so I told her I liked her shoes. I was so mad at myself. I felt so stupid. Why did I tell her I liked her shoes again?

After she finished talking about shoes, she came off the pulpit and started walking, then I heard her call my name. I was surprised; no one had ever called my name while preaching. I could not even remember if anyone had ever prayed for me after always sitting so near to the front every week. I always felt invisible, and I thought I needed more prayer than anyone else. How is it that God did not tell them to pray for me? Then again, I felt like I was living in my husband's shadow. Everything was okay with him, all dressed up in his custom-made jacket suits to fit his pride, so maybe they thought it was okay with me too.

The pastor's wife started prophesying over me that my family was on God's mind, and everyone was going to know my name; generations to generations were going to benefit from my management ability and I would be known in the gates. I sat there not knowing what to do; I just opened the palm of my hands and said, "I receive it. Thank you, God." That afternoon I questioned if it was possible for my clothing line to be known like Channel in that short period of time. That was what I had been doing at the time. I was currently going to a fashion designer class and doing my research and business plan. I decided to go do fashion designing years after trying to solve the mystery inside. I always felt like something more was out there for me than being a wife and a mother. I tried a lingerie business, which was my husband's idea, but I wasn't feeling it and I was tired of doing things people's way. I quit before it even started. Then I was his secretary, that didn't work either. I was searching for something I was passionate about; somewhere inside I felt like a creator. I thought I would be a great actress but then again maybe I wouldn't be able to remember my lines. I loved art and fashion so that was what I decided to do.

I did not know what to believe. I wondered how she knew that. I was always confused when they preached and say, "God said." Was their mind telling them that or was it that God had never talked to me before? I did not even know if He had a voice.

I can remember sometime after, the same person (pastor's wife) offended me. I was waiting in line on my turn for the pastor, her husband, to sign a book I had just purchased. It was his book, and that day was the launch. His wife started to video everyone individually and she skipped me, which seemed intentional, and went on to video the immediate person behind me. I stood there trying to figure out why she did that. I thought maybe it was because the pastor who preached that day had just used me as an example of a hot girl. After seeing her videoing her friend\amor bearer from head to shoes, in that moment, I felt like I was in high school, and they were the mean girls. I shook the thought out of my head. I went straight up, feeling confident, congratulated her husband on his book, got it signed and left. Her behavior was actually a compliment to me because if she was the leader and treated me like that, she must have seen something in me that triggered something in her.

Outside Herself

I thought about leaving the church, then told myself I was not going to give her the power over me to dislike her. I was also not going to allow her to make me leave the church because I liked the church. Thank God she was not the one preaching every week because it would have made me uncomfortable.

I left for Jamaica shortly after, spent a few weeks away and returned home. My first Sunday back home, I went to church and there she was, behind me in the greeting moment. She hugged me and said she loved me. I knew it was an apology hug.

Chapter 26

Stephen and I started making preparations to move that same year to another country, then the pandemic hit. The whole country was locked down on March 16. I remember because my birthday was the 18th. No one could leave their home, not even for church. The pastor had to start preaching from his home, so we watched it live online the following Sundays. That first Sunday afternoon, after I watched church, I sat there alone in deep meditation thinking about how people were just living their lives preparing for a next life that I was not even sure of. This did not make sense. Could I live my life feeling this way until I die and go to heaven? I never fulfilled any of my dreams and now that I was close, this pandemic came. I felt like the world was against me; I could never reach or complete anything.

As the days and weeks went by, I was starting to accept that this virus was not going anywhere so I gave up and decided I was just going to let my husband take care of me; he wanted to anyway. *I always had an independent mind, but I could not depend on myself.* I accepted it and somehow felt at ease. I started to exercise every morning; my husband would make breakfast and I made lunch and dinner. We played games now and then and kept tuned in with what was going on in the world on the news. The pandemic seemed to be getting worst as the weeks went by; thousands of people were dying all over the world; it was scary.

One night, as my husband and I was preparing for bed, he said to me, "If I die, I will be okay, but I'm worried about you."

I said, "What do you mean?"

He replied, "You don't have any faith."

It was not the first time he said that. I would normally tell him not to judge me because he could not see my heart. But how could I really have faith when nothing was right with me from I knew myself? I lived my whole life in lack. I never got what I wanted, and I never felt right. I had no hope. I wanted to cuss him out, but I was never the type to keep repeating myself, so I went to bed. I found myself thinking about what he said, and I started wondering what gave him that confidence that he would be okay if he died. *I was always afraid to die, because I have never lived.*

The next morning, I got up early before him. I went in Myles' room and sat on the carpeted floor with the Bible. I was not even sure which book I should read. I tried reading the Bible before and I did not understand it. Anyways, I opened it and it was the book of Proverbs, which I thought was the hardest based on the name of it. I started reading it and I kept reading it, even though I did not understand. I read about five chapters, then I prayed. After I was finished praying, I made a commitment that from that morning I was going to pray every day of my life, which I did. Sometimes I did not even want to get up out of bed but the commitment I made to myself made me.

One night, I dreamt I saw a word *keiken*. It was an unusual word. I had never seen that word and I had never dreamt a word before. It was very unusual. When I got up in the morning, I remembered the word vividly whereas sometimes I forgot what I dreamt about. I got up and went into the living room to get my phone which I normally left to charge overnight. I remember I went into the kitchen where my husband was and told him I dreamt a word. My husband did not dream, which I found weird. I thought it was normal for everyone to dream when you are asleep, so it was not a big deal to him, he just said okay. I then Googled the word; it was a Japanese word that means "One's own experience." I said to myself, "What was God trying to tell me?" It must have been what I was experiencing; all my life something just did not seem normal. I then wrote down the word and the meaning before I forgot it, then went on to do my usual activities.

I sat on the back patio days later strolling through Instagram search, which was unusual, when I came across an account named "womenwhosettleformore." This caught my attention, so I immediately went on the page to see what it was all about. A few videos were posted there so I started listening to them. They were about Self Leadership and Development. I was never taught these things, so I immediately started taking notes. I called Stephen and told him to buy me a notebook when he was coming home. My husband had started working after a while; he was getting contracts more than ever in the pandemic. We were blessed to be making money when some were not. I started watching the videos every day and I looked forward to them. I even ended up joining her academy.

One Sunday afternoon, I had finished cooking and sat down in the living room to watch a movie. My husband was in the bedroom resting. I got up and went to the kitchen for something to drink when I saw some water on the floor. I was not sure where the water was coming from, but I thought it was from the cases of water that were stored on the kitchen floor. I called Stephen and told him. He looked and realized that the whole yard was full of water, and it was coming in through the back door. It was raining all day but not hard. I ran and got some towels and sheet and threw them on the floor to absorb the water when I heard Myles saying out loud that water was coming through the front door also. We had to be elevating the furniture so they could not get wet. It was so sudden and shocking. It was the first time it ever happened. The whole place got flooded out that evening.

Stephen called a friend of his to ask if we could stay at his house that night because no hotel was opened. They were all closed because of the pandemic.

We ended up spending about a week until the place dried up and the carpeted floor was replaced with tiles. When I went back, the place was even painted over. My husband owned a construction company, so it was not hard to get it done in such a short time. When I went back home, the place looked new. My bedroom furniture was replaced. I then went and bought nice curtains to replace the blinds, and everything just felt new and bright. I felt like everything in my life was changing for the better. I was slowly creeping into myself as everything felt brand new. Things I wanted to get rid of for a long time were gone. Thankfully there were no more carpets because I think they were contributing to my sinus problems and Myles' asthma. I felt like the flood came to clear, not to destroy.

Now I feel like I should clear my mind. I had told Natasha about a girl I saw on the plaza on one of my last visits and told her about an encounter that we had. I told her about the girl because they both have a similar attitude so maybe it would open her eyes to know that that behavior is no good. I told her the story passionately as if I was a storyteller, but when I finished telling her the story, I felt like I went against myself and I had given Natasha dirt to bury me. Sometimes before, Natasha had sent me a message saying, "Remember mi know things bout you" and I thought to myself "What does she know about me, not because I don't tell the world something it's a secret." I replied "What?" She then said, "Oh, that message was for my boyfriend" and I wondered, "People do that? Why would you say that to your boyfriend?" I then shook it out of my head. I couldn't live with myself, so I called Natasha and asked her if she had told the girl what I told her, which I already suspected. She said she don't remember. I told her that I was sorry I told her. Natasha replied, "Why? The girl would've done the same to you." I said, "I don't care. That just wasn't me."

I then apologized to an old school mate that I had a little misunderstanding with because of my ignorance. She accepted

Outside Herself

and I moved on.

Chapter 27

I got up in a celebratory mood one morning. It was the exact date, a year before I was admitted to the hospital for my surgery to remove the fibroid that had been a struggle. That morning I woke up like a brand new me. I normally do not feel the need to celebrate but that morning was different. I felt like I had gotten rid of something that was holding me back.

I started to wonder how I could celebrate because there was no place to go; everywhere was closed. I then remembered looking on my dining table and it looked so bare, so I decided to get some flowers and put them right in the middle. I started to think maybe I could just go and drive in my neighborhood and pick some flowers, but the Spirit led me outside my yard to get some. I went and picked what I could get, and they were not flowers, they were plants. I went back inside and put them in a crystal vase I had hanging around. I realized they were colour coordinated; they were beautiful. I then sat down and rested my eyes on them, and my lips slowly melted into a smile. Somehow, I sat there feeling so proud of myself as if I was the one who made them. I started to admire them individually, each had a unique shape, texture, and pattern. Some life lessons then started to pop up in my head. It was like a switch turned on in my head.

I started to wonder what was happening to me. I went into my bathroom and started crying and asking what was happening to me, but I loved it. It was an indescribable feeling. I then realized I was thinking and seeing things differently. I started to have meaningful conversations and I was so attentive. I remember speaking to one of my cousins around that time and I enjoyed the conversation so much; I spoke confidently. I began to enjoy speaking and loving myself. I would not mind having conversations every day. It was like I woke up from the dead and not only was I alive but everyone around me, and I gave life to everything that I looked at. I felt like I was sleeping my whole life and lived in my dreams and had woken up to who I am. I started to admire everything.

I had finally stepped into myself and started to feel connected to the universe. The concrete blindfold was broken; the light spread through my entire body, broken down all barriers of doubt and fear, lit my whole world and set me free. I was no longer in darkness. *I danced in the light of myself and twirled in every room of my body, knowing I would never stumble or fall.*

I stood tall; I was born to look up, but never to look down on anyone. We are all connected; we are one.

I started to wonder how a person could hate another. Why do we stress ourselves over external things: big house and other things? Based on how I was feeling, if I was living in a hut, it would not matter to me. My world was inside of me, and I am living in my world.

My whole life changed then. I rested in Peace, I flew in Freedom, I floated in Love, and I danced in Joy. I rocked every part of my body with my hands freely opened wide. I was in heaven; I felt heaven all over me. I couldn't wait to wake up each day to the light in me, to see the world as I am.

I started to think about Jesus and understand why He did not even put up a fight when they were about to crucify Him because that was how I felt. I felt like I would sacrifice myself to save the world because I was nothing without God. I was nothing outside myself. I was nothing without my God-self.

As weeks and months passed, I was still feeling the same way, like I was in a garden walking and talking to God. One day, I was in the kitchen cooking; my book was nearby as usual, so I was cooking and writing at the same time. I was doing this for a good while until I felt like I should rest for a minute. I went into the living room and lay on the coach. I lied on my back feeling unconditional love and really proud of myself. I hugged myself and told myself "I love you" while closing my eyes and getting lost in the love and joy that I was feeling. Then I saw like a live picture of an everlasting garden, it was like a living art; it was beautiful. All the plants were fresh and not one dried up. I started looking as far as I could see the imaginary line, then slowly coming closer to where I was looking from when I saw a little girl about the age of seven wearing a white dress with plaits in her hair. She was holding on to one of the plants that had a flower and was looking at me. She smiled and I smiled back, then I heard a voice saying, "I was always with you. I go everywhere you go. I never leave you." I took a closer look at the little girl, and it was me.

I opened my eyes and melted. It was the most beautiful feeling and things I had ever seen. I broke down crying copiously. I said "Oh my God! I was dead from I was seven years old and was in heaven and living on earth in the flesh in hell." No wonder I could not succeed; everything was so hard for me. I knew something was wrong. I had no drive or passion to work at the capacity or capability to do what I knew in my head I could. I cried and asked God, "Why did You do that to me?"

One evening, in my Self-Leadership and Development Academy, I was telling my mentor what was happening to me, and she said I found my purpose and what it was. I did not have a clue what she was saying so I just told her I was going to work with teenagers. I said it off the top of my head but deep down I never felt sure.

A few days or weeks after, I went to Myles' school to make some adjustments on his school fee slip. The accountant and I started a conversation about the pandemic, and it led up to me telling her what was happening to me. I did not go into much details but she said, "Feels like you woke up out of your sleep, right?"

I replied, "Yeah, I feel like I was raised from the dead." We laughed. We had a good conversation that day, the best conversation I have ever had.

When I was leaving, she said, "Isn't it weird how it is that time you found your purpose?"

I was like, "Right!" but I was still not sure about what my purpose was. I started to think about it, and I wondered, "Is writing my purpose?" That was what I had been doing and since then I realized that I lived my story to tell it. That was the reason I got that dream, the word, "Keiken." God wants me to write my story.

Now I did not even know how to write a book. I had been writing what was in my heart; my whole life's journey, inside and out. I got up every day and wrote. I started to feel like I was on a mountain top looking down on my journey, the unsolved jigsaw puzzle that I felt inside. Now all the pieces were put together and formed perfectly. What a journey that was. I smiled to myself when I looked down. I did not even take it seriously. I laughed and realized that everyone who I encountered was just a character in my story and they had a purpose. I appreciate every one of them; if it was not for them, I would not have this story; it would not be possible.

I called my mother and asked her why she used to beat me so much. She said she was frustrated. I told her I was writing a book and it was not favorable on her side, but I understood everything now and it was okay. We do not know it all, but I must tell my story. My mother and I have a great relationship over the years. I have never treated her like she ever did me wrong. By the way, I think she is better with adults than children.

Up to this point, I had not told my husband what was happening to me, until one Sunday, I told him, and he said, "The Holy Ghost is upon you."

I smiled and said, "He is in me."

I started to ask him questions about his experience when he got saved. Christians call it "saved." He did not have much to tell me. I would tell him about some of my experiences and how I was feeling, and he said it was because I was lost. Yes, I was lost but I told him I was glad I was because if I was not lost, I would not have had these beautiful experiences.

Every day I would see little miracles and signs; it was amazing. On Sundays, I would watch my church online on Facebook. I realized that hearts would be going up with my picture when the pastor said something, as if I was the one touching them. One Sunday, I told my husband what was going on with my iPod on Facebook and he could not understand so I showed him. He saw it and said something was malfunctioning, but deep inside I felt like I had so much love and magic and it was just manifesting.

Another Sunday we were listening to church when the pastor said, "Sometimes something has to die for you to live" and I jumped up and said "Oh my God! My grandmother died for me to live. She died on the day I gave birth!" She died two years prior on Myles' birthday.

My husband said, "No, God don't work like that."

I replied, "Jesus died for us!"

He said, "That's different."

I then explained, "I know it's different. Jesus died to save us. She didn't die to save me, but the fact that she died saved me." I did not know what to think of that, but all I could think of was, maybe I broke a curse. What started with her ended with me. We had a few similarities. I used to hope I don't end up like her. She never taught me anything because she knew nothing. I remember she told me a story that when she was small a lady put her hand on her head and from that time her life changed for the worst. Nothing grew around her. May her soul rest in peace.

On another Sunday afternoon, after we ate dinner, my husband and I sat down in the living room talking as usual and I asked him, "Don't you think I should celebrate what I'm experiencing?" He gave me an answer; I do not remember the exact words that he said, but I got the feeling or understanding that he said Christians don't celebrate that.

A few minutes later, he stepped out of the house to meet with someone, so I decided to use the time to go fold laundry. While folding the laundry, the question was still stuck in me. I remember asking, "Should I celebrate?" Then I said, "I should celebrate" and in that moment I felt the most beautiful thing. I felt my heart smile. The smile was like a heartbeat. It was a fleeting moment that made me want to celebrate. It was so beautiful, I melted into tears. It felt like a father and daughter moment I never had. I was thinking, "OMG! God smiles!" I did not know God smiled. I always thought God only gave commandments and rules and if we did not abide by them, He would punish us. I realized in that moment that I could comfortably speak to Him, just as how I would speak to my earthly father. It does not matter what language you speak; it does not matter how not smart you think you are, just speak to Him. Days when I talked and laughed with Him at simple little things, I knew it was Him. He is my Friend, and He is everything to me. I no longer feel lonely, I love being alone. Everything else is a distraction.

At times when I was writing this book, I stepped back out of myself, and that was when I felt like, "Was I really going to tell the outside world my story?" It did not feel right speaking about others, especially those who did me wrong. I prayed about it. I even asked about it, but it always came back to me saying, "It's a part of my story" and the outside world is just doubt, guilt, shame, fear, ignorance, lack, darkness; So, I stepped right back in; I loved it in here, it's where I belong. It's home, where you find true Love, Joy, Peace, Light, Creativity, Power and Wisdom. **Inside is Heaven. Outside is Hell.**

Inside was dark and empty, I didn't know I Am the light and the one to step in, to feel whole. Now I Am a Queen in my Kingdom looking through my own eyes, from above, and giving life to what I see.

I was dead, now I am alive and I am ready to live.

Unprecedented

COVID 19
Outside And Inside World

It was an unprecedented time for the world
    It was also an unprecedented time for me
The world see it as destroying times
    I see it as a building time
The world see it as a change for the worst
    I see it as a change for the best
People went into depression and despair
    I went into myself
They see darkness
    I see light
They feel sadness
    I feel love
Some dead
    I'm alive
Some sleeping
    I'm woke
Some in hiding
    I want to be seen
    I see things differently
    I'm staring in the light without shades
    and without a doubt in my mind, I'm Free
    I want to be heard, not by my voice but my words
    My words have Meaning, my words have Power
    My words are Alive
    As I'm writing this, tears in my eyes
    Because it's an unprecedented time

My life was like climbing a dark steep mountain getting sticked by thorns.
Oftentimes I looked down and saw people who even younger, moving in their flow, like a river, passing by.
And I wonder why I had to climb.
But the best view is from the hardest climb.
Don't Give Up

Sahara Patrickson Forbes

She is the darkness, I Am the light
She is the flesh, I Am the spirit

Her whole world was behind her
And she was moving towards nothing

She was moving too fast
I couldn't keep up
She was ahead of time
I was behind

She kept running from home
to find herself
But herself is home, all along

I was a shadow of my own image
I go everywhere she goes
I fade with her in the dark
I stood by her in the light
I didn't speak, because no one knew my language

Her busy mind separated us
I was so near, yet so far

I wanted to fly
But was caged in darkness
And wings were clipped by fear
I tried but kept falling
I shouted for help, but no one could hear me

She was like a lamb to her own feet

Outside Herself

To be free is to be naked. Strip yourself from all the beliefs, guilt, fear, resentment, etc. Forgive yourself and forgive others to set yourself free.

In order to grow, you have to be planted. Go within, be still and be patient with yourself, so you can grow and bear fruits to feed your people.

*Sprinkle some love everywhere you go,
so you can find your way back home.*

Acknowledgement

I am honored and humbled to be the chosen one to have lived to write this book, to shed some light on other's path for them to reach their destiny.

A huge thanks to my husband for his financial support and for God to use him to lead me; he has been the moon in my darkest nights.

To my sons who showed me love daily in their own way, my big son, Ramone, who would text me "I love you, goodnight" every night. The only regret I have was not being there for him as a mother should.

To Myles, who thinks he was born to love me. He would shout from his room "I love you mommy!" and randomly hug me as if he knew I needed it when writing my story. It wasn't easy, it was a healing process for me. I relived every moment of it. I love you both.

To my family and few friends, I appreciate you guys so much. My sister, Sancia, my mom, Jennifer, my friend, Georgette, who I talk to almost every day, and my friend, Lisa, who is like my spiritual sister, the only one in my life who always lift my spirit during our conversations with her positive vibe and remind me to not take this book lightly.

Thanks to everyone who has crossed my path and all the characters in my story; there wouldn't be a story without y'all.

To the few people who knew I was writing this book and kept checking how it was going, I appreciate you too; you guys kept me going.

Shout out to the artist from somewhere in Africa who did the illustration for the cover.

A big debt of gratitude to Crystal and her publishing team who helped to make this book come to fruition. Thank you for your guidance and patience throughout the process.

To everyone who took the time to read this book, thank you. I hope you learned something in order to make your world a better place to live in.